ODELYN SMITH

Suicide Awareness and Prevention

A parent's practical guide to identifying and spotting suicide signs in children and adolescents

First published by Self-Published 2023

Copyright © 2023 by Odelyn Smith

All rights reserved. No part of this publication may be reproduced, stored or transmitted in any form or by any means, electronic, mechanical, photocopying, recording, scanning, or otherwise without written permission from the publisher. It is illegal to copy this book, post it to a website, or distribute it by any other means without permission.

This novel is entirely a work of fiction. The names, characters and incidents portrayed in it are the work of the author's imagination. Any resemblance to actual persons, living or dead, events or localities is entirely coincidental.

Odelyn Smith asserts the moral right to be identified as the author of this work.

Odelyn Smith has no responsibility for the persistence or accuracy of URLs for external or third-party Internet Websites referred to in this publication and does not guarantee that any content on such Websites is, or will remain, accurate or appropriate.

Designations used by companies to distinguish their products are often claimed as trademarks. All brand names and product names used in this book and on its cover are trade names, service marks, trademarks and registered trademarks of their respective owners. The publishers and the book are not associated with any product or vendor mentioned in this book. None of the companies referenced within the book have endorsed the book.

First edition

ISBN: 9781739586928

This book was professionally typeset on Reedsy.
Find out more at reedsy.com

Dedication

This book is dedicated to everyone who suffers from "suicidal ideation."

Foreword

As we stand on the threshold of this crucial discourse, I find myself humbled by the weight of its significance and the urgency it demands. Within the pages of this book lies a narrative not only of concern but also of hope—a testament to the resilience we foster when facing the shadows that permeate our younger generation's mental well-being.

In my seventeen years as an educator, traversing classrooms and engaging with local communities, I've borne witness to poignant narratives, heard stories that echo the depths of despair, and shared conversations with young souls navigating the tumultuous landscape of life's adversities. It is these encounters, these poignant exchanges that have spurred the genesis of this book.

"Youth Suicide Awareness and Prevention" emerges not merely as an exposition but as a beacon, shedding light on the looming threat of suicide ideation. It stands resolute, challenging prevailing stereotypes. It seeks not only to dismantle misconceptions but to sow seeds of understanding and offer a lifeline of hope amidst the darkness.

This book isn't just an articulation of concerns; it is a rebuttal, an antidote fashioned against prevailing theories that shroud death by suicide. It endeavours to steer conversations toward proactive engagement, urging parents and guardians to be vigilant, to listen, and to engage with empathy.

More than a guide, this book is a testament to possibility—a reservoir of insights poised to equip parents with discernment and young minds with resilience. It is a testament to the belief that even within the direst moments, there exists a glimmer of hope—a belief that becomes our shared strength.

As we embark on this journey, let these pages be more than words. Let them be the foundation upon which dialogue is nurtured, understanding is

Contents

Foreword ii
Acknowledgement iv
1 Introduction 1
2 I need to tell you something..... 7
3 How do you feel? 14
4 You were happy when... 24
5 Are you happy with You? 30
6 Can we? 35
7 I need to ask you something 41
8 Since you have gone 48
9 Comfort 59
10 FAQ Youth Suicide Prevention 66
11 Conclusion 81
12 Youth Suicide Prevention help and support 99
13 Resources 104
Epilogue 107
Afterword 109
About the Author 111
Also by Odelyn Smith 113

cultivated, and hope is kindled. Let us walk together, armed with insight and compassion, toward a horizon where the shadows of despair recede in the wake of understanding and support.

With unwavering dedication to empathy and hope,

Odelyn Smith

Acknowledgement

Writing this book has been quite challenging and I thank God for giving me the strength. To my beloved family, my husband, and my inquisitive children, thank you for the patience that you have shown during my time of meticulous research as I wrote the pages of this epic book.

I extend my heartfelt gratitude to the parents with whom I have engaged in conversations about Youth Suicide Awareness and Prevention. This book is a testament to our discussions and aims to be a guiding light, offering support, and assistance when needed. I hope that within its pages, you will find practical tools and insights that will aid you in navigating difficult moments and fostering a healthier, safer environment for you and your family.

1

Introduction

This book is a practical, interactive guide for parents that will help them to identify signs of suicide. Resolving the issues that children and adolescents face is a battle. But many societies aren't prepared to resolve their issues. And some societies don't have the financial capacity to fix them. This book offers solutions. Pinpointing thought-provoking questions and suggestive problem-solving ideas is our active approach to addressing issues. The overarching aim of the questions and the statements is for Youth Suicide Awareness and Prevention. Change is the trajectory of this book as it seeks to reconfigure the mind-set of how young people think. The questions will help to determine the well-being of the young person. This book will be your parental guide on how to proceed with preventative measures. Many of us have grown up in an instant world where everything is fast: instant noodles, instant popcorn, and ready-made meals. No one wants to wait. If our super fast broadband doesn't work, it's an instant headache! Do you remember the dial-up internet? Or the Amstrad, CPC 464? Technology is more savvy and complex, requiring more of an investment of your time. Working from home has brought the office's excess luggage home. Less time to exercise as more work issues mount it eats into the precious family life. Is there a solution to the work-life imbalance? As the world speeds along, there is no time to reflect and no time to think. Parents in today's society are busy chasing hiked-up bills. Minor issues with their children surface but are often overlooked or undetected under the parental radar. As parents, we have neglected to ask important examining questions. Our children are not under constant scrutiny on a day-to-day basis. Their quirky mind-set or thought patterns do not raise the red flag. The unsuspecting parent continues life oblivious to the roots that are growing. Many young people, as well as adults, have suffered separation from a loved one due to death by suicide. Reported cases of attempted death by suicide and actual suicide are on the increase.

According to CDC's provisional data for 2022 (CDC,2022, para. 3):

In 2021, suicide was among the top 9 leading causes of death for people ages 10-64. Suicide was the second leading cause of death for people ages 10-14 and 20-34.[3]

CDC's provisional data found out that (CDC,2022, para. 10):

"Youth and young adults ages 10–24 years account for 15% of all suicides. The suicide rate for this age group (11.0 per 100,000)** is lower than other age groups.[3] However, suicide is the second leading cause of death for this age group, accounting for 7,126 deaths.[3] Additionally, suicide rates for this age group increased 52.2% between 2000-2021."

The Office for National Statistics for England and Wales (ONS, 2021, para.5) found that "Females aged 24 years or under have seen the largest increase in the suicide rate since our time series began in 1981."

The demographic group of 10 - 25 years is the particular social group with more cases on the rise. Death by suicide is a shocking and awful experience for the family and friends left behind. Often, young people believe their troubles are insurmountable, leading to suicide. The heart rendered questions of "if I had known." "Why didn't he say something? "and "They seemed so happy" are some of the questions that evolve after such a tragic event. Some of these questions remain unanswered, and their reasons are seldom known. This book guides parents, concerned family members, and friends.

As a great starting point, this book has various questions and statements for readers. The questions listed will lead to meaningful topics and thought-provoking discussions. The questions will guide the parents in their identification of the problems. Questioning is the primary tool for identifying the issues. From the onset, a gentle, step-by-step, and discreet approach will

INTRODUCTION

reveal some problems. More probing and detection will, over a long period, pave the way for communication. The family members previously separated by opinions are now actively resetting their minds. As the process repeats, progressive healthy conversations will ensue. As the cycle repeats, advanced healthy conversations will happen. Discussions will bridge the gap between the adolescents' thoughts, emotions, and actions. It will help the young person stop, rearrange their minds, and release baggage. This book will change a mind of fear to a mind of peace. Rifting families will join together to resolve issues by applying the principles outlined.

Adults have all experienced dark days growing through adolescence. Some adults are odium to their teenage experience. They block out the shame and pain that they had during those years of growing. Some of us have kept these thoughts but have tossed them to the back of our minds. They never discussed their experiences and never got rid of the pain.

Over the years, the young people's struggle has intensified. The speed of AI and new technologies are developing faster than I can eat my dinner. Many children walk around, looking happy. "An Oscar-Winning Performance"….." Bravo!" On the outside, they have mastered their performance to reassure parents and friends. Contrasted with the inside feelings of guilt, hurt, and pain. They would like to tell you, but they fear what you may think! They are so scared of what they are thinking.

SUICIDE AWARENESS AND PREVENTION

It is time to break that cycle of hidden pain and guilt that wells up in your mind by talking about it. Break free from the cycle; it's time to talk. It's time to encourage your child to reach out to grab a new vibe and walk with pep in their step. Daily renewal of the mind means it's an upward battle; if you keep going, the load will get lighter. Your task as parents will be to coax and cajole them into trying something fresh and inventive. You are what you think, so do exciting and rewarding things. Consider buying your child an entirely new wardrobe of clothes and cook your child's favourite meal for the rest of the week. Book the holiday to the location the teenager has always wanted to travel to! This book will help adolescents defeat the taunting giants in their minds. Eradicating pain cycles and reoccurring negative thoughts is not a manageable condition to stop. Whether or not parents need to seek healthcare professionals' help is something to consider as events unfold. Reversing their fearful thoughts and building resilience are crucial. Children and adolescents will stop inner struggling and deflate their thoughts of discouragement. In time, young people will "Stop" the dark thoughts and prevent the acts of suicide.

INTRODUCTION

How to use the book?

The notes below are the author's suggestions on how to use the book. Remember, it is a guide; if you have a preferred method that works, please use it. Adapt the ideas to fit the various scenarios. As you read the book's sentences, take your time and mull over the words in your mind. Use a highlighter to enhance the relevant sentence selections. If you prefer to underline, do so, then stop and perpend. Time is the most essential ingredient to pinpoint the varying problems. Make the sentences your key by using different coloured highlighters. Write notes in the margins of this book and adapt them for your daily use. Purchase a diary or a journal to write or to draw your thoughts. Record the problems or the issue under your chosen headings and subheadings.

Create a timeline from today and for the next four weeks. Write down weekly dates when you intend to address the highlighted problems. Utilize the extra space at the end of each chapter under the heading of **Notes.**

Use these lines to write your thoughts or summarise each chapter's main points. Your initial notes will be the foundation of pivotal problems. Notes are the building blocks for the **Plan of action.**

The **Plan of action** section will grow and develop as you continue to read this book. Synchronize your initial thoughts with each problem, then write strategies on optimisation. Parents must slow down and commit more time to their child's developing mind. Remember when you were learning to cross the road: Rule 1 is to "Stop," Rule 2 is to "Look," and Rule 3 is to "Listen." Use the same "Stop, Look, and Listen" rules and apply them to this situation. Your child requires time and dedication to their thoughts and actions. Death by suicide is a real issue that can affect all our lives. The valuable content of this book will equip parents and increase awareness.

SUICIDE AWARENESS AND PREVENTION

Notes

Plan of action

2

I need to tell you something.....

"I need to tell you something" are comforting words parents can say to their distressed child. This chapter outlines many issues facing children and adolescents in society today. From the perspective of a concerned parent, the reader can use the suggestions. Among teenagers, suicide is more prevalent because they believe they can't overcome problems. What is the problem? Let's define what the word problem means.

"The Oxford Learner's Dictionary defines the word 'problem' as "a thing difficult to deal with or to understand,' such as 'big/serious/major.'"

The adult's perspective of a problem

Adults are more accustomed to approaching problems as hurdles. To achieve the next goal, one must overcome the hurdle. Adults are more acquainted with life battles and encounter them daily. The method and the mind-set combined can be effective problem solutions for life's struggles. Problem-solving can be inherent. Adaptation to habitat and circumstances are also factors.

The following chapter are sentences that you can use as a guide to reassure the young person. Concerned parents and friends can select relevant sentences from the list of sentences. The alternative will be to create your sentences.

"I need to tell you something…………." is an urgent message. It is necessary to have these conversations with the young person. These are essential conversations that will put the adolescent at ease. These sentences will rejuvenate the young person, adding value and care. "I need to tell you something…………." is an adult action towards unravelling the layers of pain and trauma.

I need to tell you that you are special to me and the family; you mean the world to us. I understand you tried your best when you failed your Math test, which is fine with me. It is important to me to let you know how special you are to us as a family. Don't worry; there will always be another test.

I NEED TO TELL YOU SOMETHING.....

I need to tell you that when you were a baby, you were so cute. I need to tell you how beautiful you are. Remember that your family loves you. When the school bullies call you names and say horrible things to you, this means they are jealous of you. Hold your head up high and continue to be bold. Words cannot harm you. We can talk together to work out ways to reduce and eradicate self-harming practices.

I need to tell you that although you don't match the looks and the figure of the model on your phone, you remain cherished by the family. I need to tell you that you are a Princess. Even though we don't have much money, our gift was when you were born; you are our prized possession. We value you so much, and I want you to know that.

I need to tell you that you are a creative thinker, and you can develop these talents to become an entrepreneur. You analyse and sum up situations, and this is your natural skill.

I need to tell you that even though we argue and don't see eye to eye on many occasions, I still love you. As you grow older, I hope that we can become closer in our relationship. You will be successful in life when you pursue your goals.I need to tell you that we love you more than your followers on Facebook. We can be more sociable with you if you only give us a chance to get close to you.

I need to tell you that despite having red hair, you are still handsome. Ignore the comments about the colour of your hair and the freckles on your face. Ignore the laughter, be bold and robust, and dream and achieve.

I need to tell you that money grows on trees, and one day, you will grow your tree bank. I need to tell you how we survived in the last country and will continue to survive in this country together.

I need to tell you that after spending hours of practice for your music exam and you didn't pass, you are not a failure. You are still able to retake the exam and reach your next goal. I need to tell you that life has its hurdles, and you must learn to tackle each situation. Jump over life's hurdles and continue to face the next hurdle. Life is not smooth and plain sailing; you must learn how to tackle each situation.

I must tell you that even though you look underdeveloped now, you'll blossom like an elegant rose one day. You will look more beautiful and radiant than the girls around you.

I need to tell you that the spots on your face are not a permanent facial feature. Don't feel disheartened. We can look for a cure that can dissolve them.

I need to tell you that even though everyone around you has a girlfriend or a boyfriend and you don't, this doesn't matter. As a family, we can give you more genuine love than anyone else can offer when you are an adolescent. We are the love bank. We give out love and expect no returns. Focus on your studies, discover who you are, and build confidence.

I need to tell you that being a single mother is not the end of the world. It is the beginning of the little ones' lives; lean on us, and we can do this together.

I need to tell you that even though you steal and lie to feed your drug habit, we still love you. As parents, we commit our lives to supporting you through the journey to recovery. Stay connected to us so that we can finish this together.

I need to tell you that rape is awful, and it was not your fault. You have been bold in revealing what has happened, and that is the first step. It's time to talk things through. I can get professional help if you would like for that to happen. We love you and will support you always.

I need to tell you that when you are rarely on time for school, your tardiness affects your performance. It is imperative to practice and develop organisational skills. Organisation takes time, let's plan together so that when you arrive at school, it will be on time. With the right equipment, your learning experience will become more relaxed and enjoyable.

I need to tell you that you shouldn't worry and feel isolated because the children in your class call you names. Having bad breath is a common problem; this is a curable condition. Over-the-counter treatment can used to resolve this problem. Some stores have mouthwashes that freshen your breath. We can work on getting a cure for you so you don't feel alone. You are special to me; our entire family means everything.

I NEED TO TELL YOU SOMETHING.....

I need to tell you that even when you don't fit in with other teenagers at the church, you become the leader. Being left out of conversations is an upsetting thing to happen, and this is a bullying tactic. Don't get upset with these actions and feel bitter and alone. You belong to a loving and caring family, so do not worry about their cold actions.

I need to tell you that having big feet does not mean you are a misfit, nor does it mean you are unlucky. Having big feet often correlates with having a generous heart. We can purchase custom-made shoes and trainers for teenagers online. Some websites have a variety of footwear to choose from, and the designs are contemporary.

I need to tell you that the mole on your face is a symbol of your grace and beauty. Looks do not measure beauty; beauty is what is within you. Beauty is your character. It's what defines you. When someone becomes a true friend, they will not make silly comments about your mole. A true friend accepts you for who you are, not your appearance.

I need to tell you that having a food allergy is not the end of the world. Many children and adults have to eat special diets. Don't get upset and be in a mood that you can't eat the selection of food on offer at the school canteen. Work through the food groups you can eat, then cook or bake exciting and tasty dishes. Don't be sad because of your medical condition; instead, embark on a new hobby. Look at ways of keeping yourself occupied; you can volunteer at the local food bank. Think about helping others, and your problems will become smaller.

I need to tell you that when you complain and say, "Life's not fair!" start to look at the bigger picture. Look at your life from a different angle. Become a visionary, an optimist, and wish for a hopeful future. Look at situations as an opportunity and use them to your advantage.

I need to tell you that verbal abuse often makes me feel sad, too. Thoughtless words and labels should not stick. The words can't hurt you. Choose to believe in yourself, grow stronger, and become resilient. Together, we can get stronger.

I need to tell you that we can turn negative situations into positive situations. Your non-selection for the school sports team deeply disappointed you. You can choose another after-school activity to engage in to discover your potential.

I need to tell you there were better choices than spending the credit card on gaming. Denying that you had made these purchases added more problems. I forgive you. We can look at ways that you can take more responsibility for your finances. I can get a credit card for you to become more independent. We can work out ways to pay back what you have spent. I still love you and want us all to be close the way we used to be in the past.

I need to tell you that your freckles make you who you are. Your being a star is a result of your innate nature. I need to tell you that when the bullies laugh and call you spotty, don't let this affect your kind attitude. Look at your day with hope and past what the bullies say. Let the harsh words drop to the ground, and don't let them hurt you. You are very special to me and the family.

I need to tell you that we all learn in different methods and at varied speeds. If you need help understanding a topic in class, we can learn that topic together when you come home. Learning is a process; as you go through the process, you will take small steps to reach your goal.

I need to tell you that being a different race from the other children in your class adds to the diversity. The world is diverse, with multiple cultures, faiths, and people, and we all belong to the human race. Celebrate diversity and tell others about who you are and your background.

I need to tell you that suffering from body odour during your teenage hormonal years is not uncommon. Although you seem to be the pinnacle of the class jokes, ignore them. We can buy cotton clothes with natural fibres; you can increase your water intake. As a family, you mean the world to us, and I appreciate you so much; please don't worry.

I need to tell you that even though you didn't win the prize for the best-written children's story. Your story was brilliant. I have seen all the time and the effort that you have put into your writing. Stay encouraged carry on writing, and this can be a hobby. I need to tell you that you are a fantastic writer even though you feel disappointed.

I need to tell you that despite not being selected for the cheerleading squad, you continued to strive. Don't give up. The cheerleading squad is only a stepping stone to your next significant achievement. I want to tell you that you are brilliant.

Notes

Plan of action

3

How do you feel?

What is well-being? Let's define what the word well-being means. "The Oxford Learner's Dictionary defines the word 'well-being' as 'general health and happiness,' encompassing 'emotional, physical and psychological well-being.'"

This chapter provides suggestions on how to assess a young person's well-being. Parents can use the list of questions starting with "How do you feel?" as a starting point. Often, adolescents believe their troubles are insurmountable. By hiding their emotions, young people often dig a greater hole. In time, their situation worsens, and their feelings diminish. The key takeaway from this chapter is to keep them talking while you keep on listening.

How do you feel today? Do you think the same way that you felt yesterday? Or do you feel better than you felt yesterday? How do you feel today? Are you happy with yourself today or not satisfied with yourself today? Does the way people treat you bring about feelings of sadness? What triggers your sad feelings?

How do you feel about your little world? How was school today? Is there anyone who makes you feel uncomfortable? Do you experience feelings of worthlessness? What brings on these feelings? Can we work on looking at your problems? How do you feel about the children in your class? Has anyone hurt you? Did anyone kick or punch you today?

How do you feel today? Did the bullies tease you, shouting insults at you?

What did the person say? What did the person do? Do you feel stressed or afraid? No form of bullying is acceptable.

How do you feel today? Do you still need to eat your breakfast? It's your favourite breakfast of scrambled eggs, beans, and toast. What's wrong? How do you feel this morning? You didn't play basketball on the court last night. Why have you lost interest in your favourite activity? Do you have a low self-esteem?

How do you feel today? You are complaining of having a stomach ache. Is everything ok at school? How are you coping with being the new kid in the school? I know this is your first week. You don't seem to be your usual bubbly self. How do you feel today? You have overslept, and your alarm has been ringing for fifteen minutes. You look like you haven't slept. Is there something bothering you? Is everything ok at school?

How do you feel? I found a note in your satchel, and it wasn't pleasant. Who wrote that note to you? You look nervous, and you are pretty jumpy. Is everything ok at school? Let's talk and be honest about your feelings.

How do you feel about the girls in your class? Are they putting you down every time you talk? Are they saying things that hurt your feelings, or do they interrupt you whenever you speak? Are these girls your real friends? Why don't you join an after-school club? You can then befriend girls with similar interests and build up solid friendships.

How do you feel about not having an invitation to the birthday party on Sunday? Why were the other boys from the soccer club invited and you were not? Why were you left out? Was this a kind action? Should you keep those boys as your friends? Are their actions building you up or breaking you down?

How do you feel about facing the bully at school today? Every time you go on the internet, the anonymous bully shows up. The bully has shielded their identity but seems to know your social network of gaming rooms. When you play Minecraft, the person appears to be following and taunting you. Is there a teacher that we can talk to in the school? Is there a plan that we can work on together so that life can be joyful rather than fearful?

How do you feel today? I was making your bed this morning after you left for school and discovered wet bed sheets... Did you wet the bed last night? You have wet the bed twice this week...You made the excuse that you had spilt a drink on your duvet, and I believed you. Is everything ok? Please share and tell me about your school day yesterday. This is not your usual behaviour. I have noticed that you appear to lack confidence recently and are not your normal self. Please tell me the problem and how I can help you feel better.

How do you feel? I read a message on your mobile phone that could have been more friendly. It was pretty violent and nasty. Who is sending you these messages? Is this the first message that you have received? Do you know who this person is? Have you received other messages of this nature? When did these vulgar actions start?

How do you feel at the end of the school day? How do you feel knowing you walk home that long-distance yourself? Do you feel happy and confident? Do you feel safe or look over your shoulder in fear?

How do you feel when you look at yourself in the mirror in the mornings? Do you have fewer spots today, or do you believe there are more? I can book an appointment for you to see a doctor. The doctor can prescribe a cream or an ointment to remove your spots. Many adolescents experience facial spots, and this is a common problem. Hormonal change is something that we have all gone through.

How do you feel about your height today? I know that being the tallest in the class is upsetting at times. I understand that you endure people and children who point and whisper. Your clothes must be sewn especially for you, making you unique. You are a blessing to us. You can use your height and enjoy a suitable career in the future. Are you coping with your height better this week?

How do you feel, looking at your body and your weight today? Children say harsh and cruel things and can often be spiteful. Ignore what children say, and don't pay attention to the drawings they make of you. You have a great future ahead of you. We love you, and please continue to exercise and love yourself. You are a kind and gentle person who has such a lovable character. Stay strong and be bold.

How do you feel about your allergies today? Know it gets you down that you are allergic to dairy products. It is frustrating when you must understand what you can and can't eat. Understand that you can't eat ice cream and drink milkshakes like the other children. Sometimes life is tough, but keep on going. We can buy you vegan ice cream and vegan milkshakes, too. There are many more things that you can buy to eat from the stores that are coconut-based.

How do you feel today? I hope that you had a more relaxed and calm. How has your interaction with your siblings been lately? Do you have more personal space? Can we live in peace and harmony together? Can we have another day like this tomorrow?

How do you feel about spending less time on social media? How do you feel about the reduced hours using Instagram? Are you reading more books and eBooks instead? Are you listening to calmer and more uplifting music instead of watching a thread of TikTok videos? Are you having positive thoughts this week? Do you believe that positive thoughts lead to positive actions?

How do you feel being deaf (signing)? Tell me about the good days and how you feel. How do you feel about yourself? Are you happy with yourself, or do you feel times of sadness? Tell me about your good days; tell me about your bad days. Do you feel sorry for yourself when other children call you names and make fun of you? How do you feel when the children in your class refuse to play with you? How do you feel being alone in the playground?

How do you feel about your parent's divorce? What are some of the sad thoughts that you have? Do you have any good thoughts? Do you blame yourself for the divorce? Would you feel guilty about the divorce? Can you talk to your parents about the divorce? How do you feel when you speak with your friends about your parents? Do you talk with your siblings about the divorce? How do you all feel about it?

How do you feel after the tragic accident death of your pet cat? How do you feel when you wake up, and she is not on your bed? How do you feel when you arrive home from school, and she isn't there to meet you? How do you feel when you go shopping and no longer buy cat food? What good memories can you remember? How do you feel when your friends ask about her at school? What have you said to your friends? How do you feel when you speak about her to family members? How do you feel? Are you coping with your loss?

How do you feel knowing that your Mum is dying of cancer? Do you feel shocked about your Mum having cancer? How do you feel about your Mum having cancer? Do you believe it? How do you feel about your future? Are you feeling anxious because you don't know the cause? How do you feel today? Are you experiencing sadness because you love your Mum? How do you feel when you think about your Mum? Are you feeling sorrow, pain, or distress over this situation? Do you feel grief? Do you experience grief when you think about your Mum? How are you coping with your feelings? Are you angry because you don't want this to happen to your Mum? Do you feel afraid of the future? Do you experience frustration because you cannot change her condition? How do you feel today? Are there feelings of guilt because, on reflection, you remember how naughty you were in the past? How do you feel remembering the times when your Mum cried because of your bad behaviour? How do you feel? Do you feel withdrawn and you don't want to talk with anyone? How do you feel at school? Do you feel isolated and alone, like no one around you will understand? Do you want your friends to know? How do you feel about that? Do you feel as though you are coping with the situation? Do you need help with your coping strategies? Do you need extra support? How do you feel about cancer charities and other people who have gone through this before? How do you feel about chatting to someone who has gone through this before? How do you feel about speaking to your Mum about your feelings?

How do you feel about your Dad's drug problem? Do you feel confused about the situations that you see? How do you feel when his behaviour is not normal? How do you feel when drugs are of a higher priority than the family? Do you feel betrayed when he breaks his promises to you? How do you feel about your future? Are you feeling unstable with the home environment? How do you feel when you see him lying on the floor? Do you feel anxious because you don't understand his actions or way of life? How do you feel about your Dad's behaviour? Do you feel guilty? Do you blame yourself for his way of life? How do you feel today? Is it a feeling of anger towards your Dad because your friends' dads do not behave in the way that your Dad does? How do you feel? Are you feeling resentment of the fact that he is your Dad? Do you have feelings of resentment toward your because of his drug problem? Do you have a continual low mood cycle? How do you feel about paying the household bills and looking after your younger siblings? How do you feel when you go to school? Do you feel alone? How do you feel when other children make jokes about your Dad's behaviour? Is this the reason why you misbehave in class? Do you feel as though you need to get the teacher's attention? Or is it because you are defending yourself against the comments? How do you feel when you receive low test results? How do you feel when you can't concentrate at home to complete homework? How do you feel when your books go missing, and sheets of paper are missing from your exercise books? How do you feel mentally? What emotions do you have towards your Dad? Do you want to talk with someone about your Dad's drug problem? How do you feel about talking with your Dad about his drug problem?

How do you feel about your new class teacher? Is your teacher like your previous teacher? Do you feel comfortable approaching the teacher if you need help understanding classwork? Are you receiving similar treatment to the other students in your class?

How does it make you feel when you receive punishment in class for something you haven't done? Do you think that it is fair treatment? Do you sense that you are being singled out for mistreatment? How do you feel every time this happens? How do you feel about talking with your teacher about what you experienced?

How do you feel about moving home? Do you feel happy about moving out of your neighbourhood? Do you feel sad? How do you feel about leaving your friends behind? Will you miss them? Will you continue to keep in contact with them? How do you feel about making new friends? Are you feeling a bit scared? Do you feel alone and unsure about yourself? How do you feel about moving so far away from the family? Do you want to move away? Have you spoken to your parents about how you feel? How do you feel about a smaller-sized home? How do you feel about packing? Do you need to keep everything which is in your room? What toys will you bring?

How do you feel about your physical appearance? Do you feel happy? Are you sad and embarrassed about your face? Do you like the way that you look now? How do you feel when you look at your braces? Do you feel happy, or are you feeling a bit shy? Now that you have a brace on your teeth, there are restrictions to the foods you can eat. How do you feel when you are speaking? Are you happy with the new way that you sound? How do you feel about your new look? How do you feel when people look at your mouth when you speak? Are you worried about your treatment by the other children at school? How do you feel when they do call you names? How do you feel? Are you coping with this situation?

How do you feel now that you have stopped shoplifting? How did you feel when you took your first item? Did you feel excited and thrilled that you didn't get caught? Did you feel tense and remorseful about your actions? How do you feel when you look at the items that you have stolen? Do you feel happy or sad with yourself? How did you feel when you got caught? Did you feel sad? Or did you feel relieved? How did you feel when you got arrested? Are you ashamed of this experience? How did you feel when your parents arrived at the Police Station to collect you? How do you feel that your siblings know about your habit? How do you feel that your friends at school know about your habit? Have their actions changed towards you? Do you care? Do you want to change? How do you feel about talking to someone about shoplifting and preventative methods?

How do you feel about having an operation? Is this something that scares you? How are you coping with your emotions? How do you feel about the procedures in preparation for the operation? How do you feel about losing so much time from school? How do you feel about missing out on the graduation party? How do you feel about telling your friends about your condition? How do you feel? Are you happy or sad? How do you feel about talking with a health professional about the operation?

How do you feel about not getting the job? Do you feel disappointed and sad? Do you feel ashamed of yourself? Do you feel like you want to give up? How do you feel? Do you have negative thoughts of failure? How do you feel after you have tried your best? How can you make improvements to your interview skills? Did you feel nervous and forget vital information? How do you feel about not being able to work? How do you feel about preparing for another job interview? Do you need to learn more interview techniques?

How do you feel about failing your exams? Do you feel upset and angry with yourself? Are you blaming yourself for failing? How do you cope with failure? How do you feel about retaking the subjects? Do you usually perform well in an exam? How do you feel about your results compared to other students in your class? Can you achieve your academic goals? How do you feel about implementing a study plan before the following exams?

How do you feel about your Dad losing his job? Do you feel sad about him losing his job? Do you feel happy that you see more of your Dad? Do you feel like the whole world around you is changing? How do you feel about not going on holiday this year? Are you disappointed and feeling betrayed? Do you feel the family has to move home due to the job loss? Do you feel sad that you will be moving away from your friends? Do you feel resentment that you will have to leave your school? How do you feel? Are you feeling withdrawn and unsure about yourself?

How do you feel about going to see the dentist? Do you have a fear of going to the dentist? How do you feel when you think of your past experiences? Was the experience terrible? Was it painful? Do you feel apprehensive when you hear the various sounds? What do you think when the dental instruments scrape against your teeth? How do you feel when you know that you have an appointment?

How do you feel about going to the church today? How do you feel about your friends there? Are they friendly? Do you feel as though they are true friends? Do you enjoy the church environment? Do you feel secluded and alone? How do you feel when the children ignore you? When others exclude you from conversations, how does it affect your emotions? How do you feel when the children sit in a group and leave you alone? How do you feel when you don't fit into a social group? When people instruct you to go away, how does it make you feel?

How do you feel during the autumn and winter months? Do you have happy moods or sad moods? Do you feel as though you want to stay in bed? Do you sleep for longer than average and find it hard to get up in the morning? Do you find it difficult to concentrate during the winter months? Do you feel alone and withdrawn during this time of the year? Do you experience tearfulness?

Do you find yourself more irritable for no specific reason? Why do you think you feel this way?

Notes

Plan of action

4

You were happy when...

You were happy when we went to the seaside on our last family holiday. I remember seeing you wadding into the lukewarm water. I remember the water fight you had with the boys from the family sitting next to us. I remember your laughter. I remember seeing the joy on your face when they retreated to their home base in defeat. You were happy that summer.

You were happy when you entered the ballerina competition. I remember that you practiced until your feet were sore. I remember that you competed against other schools. I can recall each team during those tense moments when somebody read out the runner-up teams. I remember seeing you jumping up and down as the second runner-up teams were announced. I remember your school team winning the first-place award in the competition. You were happy then. You all received the imitation silver medals.

You were happy at the age of five when you learned how to ride your bike without stabilisers. I recall watching you struggle at first. I remember you began to maintain your balance on the bike. I watch you as you navigate corners without losing your footing. I remember seeing your sense of achievement. I remember you holding your thumbs up and shouting, "Yes, I can do it; I can ride my bike!"

You were happy when you got a place at your high school. We went out and bought the uniform. You were so excited when you tried it on in the store, and you looked at yourself in the mirror and smiled. You looked at me and smiled in approval. You chose your school bag and the pencil case's matching stationery. You were so happy that your best friend was going to the same high school as you. You were so happy then...

You were happy when we bought the golden Labrador as a puppy; you screamed and laughed as the dog licked your face. I remember the first walk that the dog took you on. You struggled to gain control as the dog walked through your legs. I remember the dog took off pursuing a football that children were kicking around. You were happy with your dog. You were so glad when you bought the dog food and wanted to carry the heavy sack to the car. You took care of the dog, and you showered the dog with your love...you were happy then.

You were happy eating your favourite meal: cheese, tomato pizza, and fries. You used to add too much ketchup and barbecue sauce to the fries. You would make this meal last so long and savour every mouthful. Every time you ate your favourite food, I recall you used to hum a tune and bounce your legs in enjoyment. You loved that meal.

You were happy when you attended the athletics club. I remember that you were a member for three years. You would train with your local club twice a week. I remember you running with spiked training shoes for the first time. You ran like lightning. Your nickname was "Bolt" because the other members could see how fast you could run in the 100 metres. You enjoyed your time with the athletics club. You were happy then...

You were so happy when you told the family that baking would become your new hobby. It made you feel meaningful and happy when you ordered your chef hat and apron from Amazon. I watched you as you organised the kitchen and prepared the ingredients. That afternoon, I saw the customary army of hundreds of shortbread cookies cut out. You were happy because they were your favourite. Adding extra butter was a bad habit. Using your finger, you always sample a large part of the dough mixture in the bowl.

You were happy when your poem won the competition and got published in the local newspaper. You combed your hair for half an hour and modelled and re-modelled your hair with gel. I shouted at you because you had brushed your teeth so much that your gums began bleeding. You were happy then. You looked so smart, and we were so proud when you took the official photograph for the local newspaper.

You were so happy spending the weekends with your Dad. You were a pro at sorting and packing your clothes, and it was all systems go, and on the dot at 7 pm every Friday, you were ready. You were so happy when you instructed me to have fun and stay safe.

I laughed at the role reversal. Your Dad would spoil you and give you everything you asked for. I could perceive the joy. You would recount the events in excitement, and I could hear the high pitch in your voice. Repeating the weekend's activities and the adventurers you had met made you happy.

You were so happy when you learned how to swim. During the lesson, you were all instructed to remove the armbands. Under supervision, you sliced a path through the water with your hands while flailing your legs. You splashed everyone as you swam past them. I remember that day as you shouted from the swimming pool, "I can swim, I can swim." I stood up and clapped as other parents looked on and laughed. I remember your swirling motion in the water as you held up your hands and shouted, "Yes, I can swim."

You were so happy when you got your first job. You compiled the experiences that you had when assisting the elderly neighbours. You wrote down your experience of delivering newspapers from the local store. You were so happy when you opened the email and read the job offer. I remember how you laughed and started singing some money song. You told me that you would be self-sufficient and that we wouldn't need to spend a penny more on you, and then...

You were happy when you played for your school's football team. You ran into the room and chanted, "I am the best, I did it, I am the best, I did it!" You were so happy that they chose you to be captain. You were delighted to serve your team. You rallied around them, giving support and encouragement. You were pleased as you shouted "Goal. I remember you practicing running onto the ball and scoring goals in the back garden. The school was proud of your achievement, too. The head teacher wrote an article about you in the school newsletter. You were happy practicing every day after school and on the weekends. Football was your life. You were happy then.

You were happy when you met up with your cousins. You would always tell your younger cousins silly stories that didn't make sense. I remember after they listened, they would roll around in laughter. They loved to hear you. You were happy as you spoke with the different accents and acted out each role. You loved to watch cartoons with them. Or you would chase them in the garden to give tickles until they fell in a heap of laughter. You were happy then.

You were so happy when I brought you to the zoo at the age of five. You talked about that day for months until your birthday arrived. At that time, tigers were your favourite animal, and you begged me to walk past the section five times. You photographed lots of tigers and too many photos of me. You were happy as you called out to the tigers; you even gave them names as you pointed to them. We ate fish and chips and had too much ice cream at lunch. You said, "Today was the best day ever!" I saw the gleam in your eyes and heard the excitement in your voice. I can't remember when this gleam faded, when this happiness left you.

You were so happy when we bought you a mountain bike for your fifteenth birthday. You were silent for about 10 seconds before walking forward to take the handlebars because it was the mountain bike you had requested. I remember the first stunt that you performed. You tilted onto the back wheel, lifted the front wheel off the ground, and shouted at the top of your voice. The neighbourhood kids came and watched you in awe. You rode away and returned two hours later. You were so happy then.

You were happy playing Mary in the school's Christmas Nativity Play. At home, you rehearsed your lines over and over again. Even your younger sister knew your lines! You played the part quickly and were so happy when you held the toy baby Jesus. You were delighted when you spotted us in the crowd, waved, and forgot some of your lines. You were happy when you sang in the play with your classmates. At home, you shared your production blunders. You were happy that we had seen your performance.

   You were happy when you went fishing with the family every Sunday. You loved making your favourite jam sandwiches in the morning. You enjoyed packing the car with the fishing nets, the fishing rods, and the tripods. You wanted the competition to be the first to catch a fish. You would be extra happy if you won. You received a Samsung phone for Christmas. I remember you photographed everyone and anything that moved while fishing. I remember you saying that you wanted a career in photography.

You were happy when we went to Disneyland, Florida. You were so excited and told all your classmates. You planned your visits, and Animal Kingdom was at the top of your list. When you arrived, you collected the Disneyland guide in multiple languages. I remember the guide in Spanish, French, Italian, Mandarin, and many other languages. When you returned home, you wanted to keep them all in a keepsake box. As you queued for the rides, you took out the guides and tried to read what they said in the different languages. You were happy when you got to go on the Disney Safari ride and went on it four times during the day. By the fourth time, you knew the script of the Disney attendants and would say it simultaneously. You were happy then…

You were happy when you entered the School's Master Chef Competition. You were happy as you planned to cook your favourite dish, "Ackee and Saltfish." Months before, at home, you would prepare the ingredients. You were happy when you cooked this meal five times the week before the competition. You were happy because you had timed everything with meticulous precision. You came third in the contest and were still happy with the outcome. You were happy as you retold how the judges loved the spices and the wonderful aroma you had created. You were happy when your classmates fought to get a mouthful at the end.

Notes

Plan of action

5

Are you happy with You?

Well-being is an important aspect that you want to assess. As a parent or guardian, you can observe the child's or adolescent's well-being. You can identify things and flag them up during conversations for further review later. Well-being is not tangible, so you need to understand what to look for in your evaluation. According to the Oxford English Dictionary, online Well-being is: "Concerning a person or community: the state of being healthy, happy, or prosperous; physical, psychological or moral welfare." "Concerning a thing: good or safe condition, ability to flourish or prosper."

Under a variety of categories, Well-being is a state of being healthy. From the perspective of a parent, you are assessing many things. You are looking for signs of happiness or the contentment the child usually exudes. You are looking for actions of comfort and security traditionally shown by the young person. You are looking at their physical posture, whether it is the same swanky walk with the shoulders back. You will be observing their emotional state and psychological state of mind. As a parent, you will be more aware of the young person's standards. You will be looking at their quality of being, whether excellent or satisfactory, with their life. Throughout this chapter, you can ask a young person a range of questions. These questions are only starting points; you may have your questions. Use the Notes section to write your thoughts and questions. Highlight the relevant questions from this chapter that you would like to use.

ARE YOU HAPPY WITH YOU?

Are you happy with you? What thoughts are going through your mind when you wake up in the mornings? Can you recall any thoughts that you had before you slept? Do you sleep? Or are you lying awake at night? Do you look at yourself in the mirror? Do you like how you look in the mornings? What are the inner thoughts that you have in the morning? Do you like how you look in the mornings? Are you happy with how you feel in the mornings? Do you think life has been good for you?

Are you happy with you, or do you feel uncomfortable around people? Do you feel uncomfortable around teenagers in your age group? Why do you feel uncomfortable? Are you a friendly person? Are you an approachable person? Do you approach and try to communicate with other teenagers? Do you accept that teenagers are different? Do you feel uncomfortable because of these different characteristics?

Are you happy with you? Do you have self-confidence? Do you think that other adolescents enjoy being around you? Do you radiate warmth so that others want to be near you? Do you think the children talk down to you and play the belittling game whenever you are present? Is this the way that all young people speak to you? Does this person shout at you when you try to converse? Does this person talk over you during the conversation? Do you feel that others treat you respectfully? Also, please let me know if you need any spelling, grammar, or punctuation errors. Do you feel uncomfortable around anyone else?

Are you happy with you when you think about your past? Are you happy when you remember your living environment? Do you believe that your past moulds your future? Are you thinking of your past in a good or bad way? Are you carrying a burden of guilt and shame? How are you copying when you think about your harsh treatment in the past? Do you want to talk about your past? Do you want to talk about anything that bothered you?

Are you happy knowing the teacher has not supported you in the classroom? Are you satisfied speaking with the teacher? Do you think that the school has failed you? Are you completing your work in the classroom? Are you happier when you sit alone at the table in the class? Does the teacher assist you if you ask for help? Are you happy being alone during the school day? Is this your coping strategy to get through each school day?

Are you happy with you? Do you consider the speaker or the content of the words? Do you believe everything that other young people say to you? Are these words of affirmation? Or are they words of degradation? Do you believe in yourself? Will you achieve your academic goals? Do you think that when you leave school, you will be successful? Are you happy with yourself in the way you think?

Are you happy with you when you don't tell the truth? Are you happy with your life? Are you happy with the lies that you have spun? Are you telling lies to cover up your true feelings? Do you believe the lies that you speak? Are you happy with the lies and their outcomes? Why do you avoid the truth? Is facing the truth hurtful? Are you more comfortable when you tell a lie about your problem? Are you happy when you are in these situations? Are you searching for a resolution for your pain?

Are you happy with you? Are you feeling more anxious? Why do your anxious thoughts appear natural? Should you trust your judgment? Should you trust your thoughts? Is this something that you have experienced for an extended period? Do other young people and adolescents go through similar feelings?

Are you happy with yourself? You seem underweight. The trousers that fit you well are now hanging off you. Are you eating breakfast, lunch, and dinner every day? Are you eating a healthy breakfast in the morning to start your day? Are you waking up in time to eat a breakfast? Are you eating lunch when you go to school, or are you snacking on crisps and candy? Are you happy with the way that you eat? Are you satisfied snacking instead of eating a well-nourished meal? Are you eating your dinner when you go to your Grans after school? Are you happy when I prepare your favourite meal?

Are you happy with you? Are you happy with your academic performance? Do you compare yourself with other young people? Do you think that you are as brainy as your peers? Are you happy with the high expectations that you place on yourself? Do you compare your life and your household environment to others around you? What are you comparing? How do you feel after each comparison? Can you change what you are measuring the success against? Should you believe the outcomes?

Are you happy with you? Are you uncomfortable with anyone in the family home? After your grandma's birthday party, you seem a lot quieter. Has something happened? Has a family member said something upsetting to you? Is there a reason why you left the celebrations early? Can we discuss this in more detail now or when your father arrives home? Do you need to learn skills on how to deal with toxic family relationships? Are you happy with your family ties?

Are you happy with you? Since you entered the "Talent Contest," you have become quieter. Are you happy with the other competitors? Did you experience a change in behaviour towards you from other contestants? Have you experienced jealousy and harmful actions? Are you happy with the way that the competition is going? Did others feel threatened by your success? How have you learned to cope with success? Are you happy to learn methods of growing your talent?

Are you happy with you? Is speaking something that you have found to be a challenge? Are you afraid of saying the wrong things? What are your reasons for not talking? Are you unhappy when someone mocks what you have said? Are you afraid because you are fearful of this happening? Are you happy when you are silent? Do you want to experience freedom from self-doubt? Are you happy with your feelings? Is expressing yourself hard to do? Why do you think your communication is wrong? Are you happy when you communicate well?

Are you happy with you? Are you making good decisions daily? Are you succeeding after making these choices? Do you have a sense of peace as you plan? Are your choices beneficial to others around you? Are you bothered about the people around you? How can your parents support you in the future? Are you willing to listen to their ideas? Have your decisions made a positive impact on your life? Are you making good decisions that will help you to succeed?

Notes

Plan of action

6

Can we?

"Can we?" is the start of the questions in this chapter. The invitation word 'Can' is a verb that signifies taking action. It's a prompting word that can also mean whatever task is achievable. Parents are guiding the young person into accepting one of the invitations. The young person starts to engage through agreement, which is a positive response. They are not obliged to. The word 'we' means the request is not for individual participation. It is for joint involvement. Parents may give the request to the adolescent, even if they might not receive it. The parental process of asking their child questions through invitations and taking action requires patience. Asking the "Can we?" questions are the first step, so the next step is to use a minute amount of coercion. Be persistent and develop resilience. The willingness to participate can take time because of their mind-set. There will be rejections, but only for a period of a while. Your efforts will help to untangle the thoughts of the mind. Finally, the release and the process of restoration will begin.

Can we find a way to overcome your claustrophobia? A student locked you in the janitor's cupboard in primary school. You experienced high levels of fear and anxiety, and you felt embarrassed by the incident. Your self-confidence plummeted, and it caused negative emotions. Your challenge is to focus on happy memories. Overcoming your fear is essential. Can you breathe slowly and count to three with each breath? Can we book an appointment together to see a health professional? Can we find a solution for your claustrophobia? Can we walk the dogs together? Conversations while walking the dog will allow parents and their children to brainstorm ideas to resolve the problem.

Can we speak to your subject teacher and request a meeting? Can we discuss rearranging the seating of the students in that particular class? The ring leaders in the class distract other children from learning. The class will be more settled and have a chance to learn when they are not sitting in friendship groups. After the reshuffle, you can focus on yourself and your academic progress instead of your focus being on survival tactics in a class that is not learning.

Can we work on this problem together and reduce your daily food consumption? We can adopt a new approach to eating by adding healthy alternatives to junk food. In the long term, eating a balanced diet with various fruits and vegetables will prolong your life. Your taste buds will adapt to the change of foods, and you should begin to enjoy the foods a lot more. Can we see if today there is a different atmosphere in the canteen? Try to queue towards the end after the principal offenders have gone. Sitting to eat your lunch will make you feel more at ease and not feel panic-stricken. Remember that the best way to consume your lunch is when you are comfortable.

CAN WE?

Can we spend some time together shopping for a new outfit? A bit of retail therapy is what you need. Shopping can help you to relax and will help you to de-stress. During the shopping spree, walking will enable you to exercise. The exercise combined with the shopping will help to restore a positive vibe. Afterward, we can review the matter as we sit in McDonald's and sip our milkshakes. Can we identify other areas to investigate? Good talking leads to good planning, and this leads to positive outcomes.

Can we look at ways in which you can make friends? Skateboarding is a great hobby, and you have demonstrated quite a skill. This hobby can become a professional sport. Enter skateboarding competitions so that young people will have the chance to meet other young people who share the same values and interests. Constructing sports competitions to help Prevent Youth Suicide is another initiative to reach out to adolescents across the country. Having a common ground to communicate is a starting block for a conversation. It is a starting block for a good friendship.

Can we work out ways of getting your homework done? How can we limit our time on social media each evening? I would like you to reduce your engagement to one hour in the evening. Please complete the school homework first, and then the last hour is your social media time. Can we speak together about homework time management? You have got your life ahead of you. You are good at Maths. Would you like to have a career in Maths?

Can we play Minecraft? After thrashing you in the game, we can discuss how to solve these issues. Can we walk home after school so that you don't walk alone? Can we make dinner together and discuss some finer points as we cook? Can we fix how you feel by arranging for you to visit your Dad every fortnight? This arrangement will enable you both to bond. Eradicating physical bullying is a strategy that we must tackle together. Can we examine the situation together? We can enroll you in self-defence lessons such as Karate or Taekwondo. These classes will build your self-confidence. When the bullies know that you are attending the martial arts class, this will be the catalyst for them to stop.

Can we have a chat about your problems? Each week, we can share our thoughts and experiences. Can we work together to build a good rapport? You can speak about your problems, write them down, or draw your situations on paper. Expressing your feelings twice or three times a week can help reduce your tension. I can enroll you in an after-school activity; the plan is for you to stay a bit later on the school grounds. You can then avoid the gangs of adolescents who cause trouble, and you will have an easier time as you commute home. Can we plan together?

Can we work on achieving positive outcomes after resolving your problems? Can we work together to replace your negative thoughts with positive thoughts? Can we indulge in afternoon delicacies as we confer? Your outlook on life is a reflection of how you see your life. Can we create a vision and goals to work towards? We can work on methods of radiating positivism towards your friends and family. Concentrate on self-development; you can be whoever you want to be. You can overcome your problems and change your outlook on life. Can we work on embracing change and not being afraid of change? Learn to avoid negative small talk and do not believe in jealous criticism.

Can we find ways of coping with your change in medication? According to the doctor, you will feel a lot better very soon. A change in medication will mean a change in your mood or changes in your emotions. Can we talk about how you feel daily? We can schedule brief meetings so that we can have a chat about how you feel. Can we have regular conversations about your thoughts? New medication brings new concerns; can we discuss these? We can work together in many ways to tackle the issues that affect you the most. Can we discuss the possible new side effects? Can we talk to a health professional about how we can cope with depression?

Can you use another method of gaming with your friends? The payment games are costly, and your phone bills are high. How do you feel when you run out of credit? Your actions are beginning to impede the financial well-being of your parents. How do you think that costly gaming is why your parents argue with you? Can you use a game that doesn't need a method of payment? We can look at new strategies for tackling this. We can put ideas together to construct a solid action plan. Can we discuss how you are feeling? Let's allow for a time of reflection upon your actions and the circumstances. Can we approach gaming and being social from a different perspective? Step by step, we can work together to resolve each issue.

Can we observe the situation at the school gates and the ill-treatment that you have experienced? How does bullying make you feel? How do you feel when they shout at you? Can we discuss the different ways of approaching these adolescents? Can we use the bold tactic to make ourselves appear bigger than our situation? Practice walking with your head up high and your shoulders back. Can you practice shouting "No" to a mirror. Practice shaking your head and using your hands to show gestures of disagreement. Can we adopt a new attitude to life? Can you focus on positive things until we can find a resolution?

Can we look at life in a new, uplifting way? Can we talk while we eat a cheese and tomato pizza with deep cheese-crusted edges, topped with pineapples? The challenges that you encounter can only make you stronger. Being honest is the best policy in moving forward. Release yourself from the fear of failure and begin to excel. Build your future on a solid foundation of thoughts and motivational speeches. Can you listen to motivational speeches in the mornings? Start on the right footing, and everything you hoped for will fall into place. Adopt new attitudes and improve the vision of your future. Let's discuss approaching your problems and planning for a more transparent and dynamic future. Young people should approach life with vigour and lots of enthusiasm. Can you open your mind to more significant opportunities?

Notes

Plan of action

7

I need to ask you something

I want to address the parents and friends who are reading this chapter. Some of the change has to start with you. You must develop your communication skills. When parents communicate better, you can achieve your goals more. The "Better Up" website shares advice on how to "Develop good listening skills"(2023, BetterUp).

The Samaritans website shares valuable insights on "How to develop better communication skills."

Listening and becoming an "Active Listener" are techniques that parents must learn. Future conversations will produce results. The Samaritans website was a good resource bank. The website will help you in the journey of reaching your target audience. It reveals ways of improving listening skills using the SHUSH method. SHUSH is an acronym for; S-how you care, H-ave patience, U-se open questions, S-ay it back, H-ave courage.

Learn more tips and expand your parenting skills first. Demonstrating good listening skills is an essential aspect of this process. The self-development process may take a couple of hours or a day. The process makes you more aware of what you say and how you appear so that you can excel in both areas.

Well done, you are now ready.

The title of Chapter 6, "I need to ask you something," is a profound statement or an assertion rather than a question. However, when you add a question mark on the end, it transforms into an interrogative sentence. "I need to ask you something?" Asking the statement requires boldness on the part of the questioner. In other words, you must prepare your mind for the worst possible answer. The anticipated answer may not be the answer that you want to hear. Although the outcome may be what you don't want to hear, stay positive in your thoughts. The answer given may change the course of life for the parent or friend who asks the statement. You may experience shock and distress. There may be moments of denial and disbelief. Throughout the process, you must stay focused and maximise the content you hear. After the conversation, write down what you had heard. Next, write down your feelings, thoughts, and emotions. Consider the path of parental initiative that you need to take.

This book's challenge is changing the young person's mind-set from one way of thinking to another. The purpose of this chapter is to suggest questions that parents can use in their assessment. Asking a question and receiving a response is a good outcome. In such an imbalanced world, young people are battling against more issues today. Compared to three years ago, the trepidation they encounter is enormous. Teens are more likely to take their lives due to the mistaken belief that their problems are insurmountable. In this fast-paced world, there are more demands on your time as parents, too. Since the pandemic, more parents have worked from home, and there is less work-life, home, and children balance. Young people experience more demands on their educational performance at school. Adolescents experience more complex situations in this social media-dictated society. Life has bombarded teens with issues that adults and parents can manage, but teens can't. There is no taboo about death by suicide; we should speak about it more.

Highlight the relevant questions in your child's story and their situations. These are some of the challenging questions to ask, and they may help save a young person's life. Below are some examples of how you can lead up to the question:

During the past six months, you have changed. You used to be happy and enjoyed attending school and participating in the debating society. You heard about the after-school running club. You have boasted that you had a good set of friends. You say many negative things like "Life would be better without me." You also say, "I wish I wasn't here." You have changed; you're a recluse. You refuse to go to school and are no longer interested in running. Your grades have plummeted. And you don't want to get out of bed. As parents, our concern is about your health and well-being. I need to ask you something…are you thinking of taking your life by suicide?

It has been quite a shock that your Dad has gone to prison for five years. I understand the shame and the embarrassment that you have felt, especially when it was on the local news. Your Mum spends lots of hours working and trying to make ends meet. You feel alone in the home when you arrive from school. I understand that you have undergone a lot of change recently. Your secure family unit is no longer operational. I have noticed that you are not your usual bubbly self. You don't communicate with your peers like you used to. You don't hang out with them on the weekends. You look tired… Are you sleeping at night? Are you worrying about your Dad, your Mum, your future? I need to ask you something…are you thinking of taking your life by suicide?

    I understand being the primary career for your Mum can be very stressful. Life can be pretty demanding when you are the eldest child in your family. Your

Mum and your siblings all depend on you. Organising the cleaning of the home and balancing school homework is not an easy task. The challenge is to feed your younger siblings and help them develop. You have done well, but recently, you have become withdrawn and unwilling to support your siblings. You haven't completed your home chores for weeks. Your siblings are complaining about not eating during the day. Your care of your Mum is quite haphazard, and you are not communicating with anyone. I need to ask you something...are you thinking of taking your life by suicide?

I understand that going through a change in your medication will alter your sleep. The change may also affect the way that you think. Your positive thoughts may change to negative thoughts. Your change of medication will cause you to experience mood swings. Your outlook on life will become a lot different. Remember, this is only for a short time, so this is a time of conformance. You have been negatively talking that way lately, suggesting random things. I need to ask you something......are you thinking of taking your life by suicide?

I know that you are experiencing various academic pressures in school. You are trying desperately to keep up with the trends with your peers in school. It is not easy to keep up when you hang out with the popular crowd. Other adolescents may be more influential, so competition to be the "Top Dog" can be intense. Recently, you have been making jokes about death and claiming that to take your life by suicide is a good thing. Your child may be going through pressures in school, but this is not normal behaviour. The parent should take this opportunity to ask the critical question:

I need to ask you something......are you thinking of taking your life by suicide?

I've seen how you have fought through diet after diet. You have lost weight, and then you have gained weight. I understand the reasons why you want to lose weight permanently. I have listened to you as you shared your journey and how you felt hopeless. You have discussed your doubts and fears and how you have struggled over the past five years. Understand that this hasn't been an easy road, especially when you face adverse comments. Both children and adults seem to subject you to name-calling and ridicule; you have been brave.

You haven't spoken with anyone recently and have spent the past two days in your bedroom. I need to ask you something......are you thinking of taking your life by suicide?

I understand that you experienced trauma when you left your homeland to live here. The barriers that you encountered were those of language and educational attainment. Difficulties intensified after your Dad took his life by suicide. Your Mum's primary responsibility was to provide for her five children. You have worked hard to learn English speaking, listening, and writing. I know how you have fought to gain good friendships. I haven't seen much of you lately after the diagnosis of your Mum's cancer. You haven't looked the same since you have heard the news. You don't appear to be happy anymore. You speak negatively about your life here and how life used to be at home. You joke about death and going to live in a better place. I need to ask you something......are you thinking of taking your life by suicide?

There have been many economic factors that have led to the increase in grocery prices. The petrol price has risen generally, and the cost of living has risen. People experience life filled with uncertainty and fear about the future. I know that you are very worried since your Dad lost his job. He has been applying for positions but without success. Bills are mounting, and he has no further credit available. I can see how distressed you are, and you keep talking about the family's financial problems. You look distressed and have become withdrawn. You didn't attend the school prom because your Dad had no money to pay for your dress and the meal. I need to ask you something...are you thinking of taking your life by suicide?

The sudden death of your Nan was a shock, and due to the COVID-19 restrictions, you were unable to attend her funeral. The death of your Mum a year later was heart-wrenching. How are you grieving and coping with your loss? One death in a family is not easy, but two deaths within a year is tough. You walk around the playground with your hood on your head. You appear distant but often get angry or aggressive when children approach you. How are you managing the changes in your life? Life has been quite tricky, and I am concerned about you. I watch you biting your nails and stowing away in secluded places. There are support groups that can help you through this challenging period. I need to ask you something......are you thinking of taking your life by suicide?

You have experienced a roller-coaster of emotions in your life. Your older brother applied for hundreds of engineering jobs after he finished college. He received rejection after rejection. He received rejection after rejection. He always interviewed well but was never shortlisted. He became very anxious, and his downward spiral of depression started. Your Mum reassured him that he would get the ideal job. She would encourage and talk with him. She encouraged and spoke with him. Sometimes, he would listen, but often, he sat with a blank look on his face. There was a battle in his mind. He believed that nothing good was in his life. We thought he deserved no engineering job. He took his life by suicide and wrote a note apologising for his actions. Remember, your family was shocked; the entire village came to pay tribute to his young life. We had achieved so much in school, and he was a popular character loved by the students and his teachers. Your Dad had disagreements with family members. He was defending his actions as a parent and his son's actions.

Some family members were cruel in their analysis of the situation. They concluded that your Dad had spoilt his son, while others said he was an attention seeker. Life was not fair. Your Dad seemed to wither under the strain of it all. The fees for the funeral alone emptied his bank account. After the death of your brother, Dad blamed himself for his death. He didn't want to work because he was still grieving. There were so many unanswered questions. Why did he take his life? What if he had spoken about how he felt? Could there have been a chance of him living? During the following year, his self-esteem and his confidence plummeted. Eighteen months later, your Dad took his life by suicide. Words can't express what you are going through. Words cannot replace the loss, anguish, pain, or anger you feel. I need to ask you something…are you thinking of taking your life by suicide?

Self-Development Notes

Plan of action

Notes

Plan of action

8

Since you have gone

Chapter 7 is an attempt to show how life would be for family members and friends if death by suicide were to occur. Death by suicide is the worst possible scenario. This chapter shows the changes in the lives of the family members and friends left behind—the grieving process and how a sudden death can affect everyone. Having to bury or cremate someone unexpectedly carries significant financial implications. The unexpected need to bury or cremate someone entails substantial economic consequences. Parents may feel more of a strained atmosphere in the home between the each other and the siblings. Siblings may choose to rival each other because of the position fighting. This chapter will demonstrate the pain and mental baggage that parents may start to carry. The health implications and how the depressed mind may lead to health depreciation. The author aims to show the possible negative conversations and accusations that may occur between siblings in the home. The rebuttals and the unanswered questions the emptiness, the guilt and despair that parents feel. The loneliness and the lack of joy that a friend experiences. This chapter has many perspectives. The different scenarios are from the viewpoint of the parents, siblings, and a friend. Bite-sized paragraphs separate the scenarios, making the text easy to read. You may be familiar with some problems which may be hard to digest, so please peruse the text. "Since You Have Gone" is a melting pot of intertwined emotions resulting from such a tragic event.

Since you have gone, the family has never been the same... Since you have gone, we cry at breakfast, lunch, and dinner. Since you have gone, we no longer go on our annual family camping holiday. Since you have gone, the dog has been whining and displaying signs of distress. The dog barks and looks towards the door, wagging his tail at 4 pm. That was the time that you would arrive home from school. The dog performs this ritual every day...... I know that you will never walk through the door again.

Since you have gone, I can hear our past conversations and arguments. They are all meaningless; the tattoos, the alcohol, and the girlfriend are all meaningless. Since you have gone, we don't laugh like we used to. Sometimes, we sit in silence and stare out the window. Our bodies are in the same room, but our minds are wondering, capturing a glimmer of a different ending. How life would be different if you were still here?

Since you have gone, I have walked outside in the evenings because I don't sleep as much as I used to. I am trying to sleep naturally; I find it challenging and lie awake each night, so I now depend on tablets to bring on sleep. Since you have gone, I sometimes need to remember where I parked the car when shopping. Sometimes, I need to remember where I have driven from and where I have driven to. I have to write more things down to remind myself of daily tasks. I have lost a part of me.

Since you have gone, our financial debt has spiralled out of control. I took out a loan to cover the funeral costs. There was so much to organise; the hearse, the flowers, the cremation, the funeral program. The paperwork was so draining, and there were many questions to answer so many places to bring the letter. There are many weeks of feeling tired and distressed. Forgetting vital dates and only remembering the date of death. A year later, our financial situation has worsened. We are struggling to eat, struggling to pay bills, and trying to survive. I still miss you, and I can't fill the void. My nights merge with the day because I can't sleep. I wake up in the afternoons and sleep through the mornings. I have flashbacks of good memories: your first day at school and when you learned to tie your shoelaces.

Since you have gone, your brother has never been the same. He was lively and bubbly, but his character has changed. He used to be outgoing and had a positive perspective on life. Since you have gone, he is now a recluse, reserved, withdrawn, and very quiet. I often forget that he is in the same room. Since you have gone, we haven't heard his silly jokes. I hear no laughter. Your brother has no one to wrestle with and no one to push around. He no longer runs down the stairs excitedly, anticipating hearing something new. He is lost in his thoughts and indecisive in his actions. He is like a leaf drifting in the wind falling. Every day, he asks me, "Why?" I can't answer his question because this is my question, too. In school, he plays alone, sitting on the grass, not engaging with the children around him. What a change, what a difference.

Since you have gone, the rest of the class had to have counselling for months. Your teacher cried in front of the class, and other classmates called together, too. You were the centre of attention in the class. You often entertained the class with your dry humour and wit. The teacher says she still sees students hugging each other in the corridors and crying. Children still speak about you in the classroom and on the playground, and this is six months on...

Since you have gone, I started an awareness campaign for parents to look for signs of death by suicide. My focus group is children, adolescents, and young people under 25. Since you left, I have created a website and have worked in the community to raise awareness. My future goal will be to have a charity called the "Kwambi Foundation." You enjoyed your holiday in northern Namibia, and Kwambi is the language spoken there. Since you have gone, I have helped 32 families, and more families and young people are waiting.

Since you have gone, time goes slowly. In my mind, I see you through your baby stages and hear your baby's laughter; I can listen to your cries. I can see you crawling across the carpet. I can hear you trying to talk and see you walking and running. I can see when your first tooth fall out, and the adult tooth was pushing through. I can see you when you were 13 years old... I can see you in my mind as if you continued to grow through the different stages of life. I picture you in your adult life and think about the type of job that you would have had. I tried to envisage your first girlfriend, your first car, and our grandchildren. Since you have gone, I get tired of thinking and wondering. I am tired of crying and trying to undo life...

Since you have gone I see more of my estranged brothers and sister who never came to visit. They stay for long periods, two hours or an entire afternoon! At first, I felt uncomfortable talking and reminiscing about the good old days. I felt guilty about reflecting on funny events that had happened in the past. Talking brings a glimmer of peace, an element of healing. There are still days when I would instead escape and go shopping. The family togetherness has helped. We get on a lot better. I visit them too, and sometimes we have Sunday dinner together. Chapters in our lives are missing due to the years of separation. Since you have gone, my siblings have tried to play a catch-up game of family ties. Sometimes, we don't see eye to eye, but when we leave the home, we say positive things to each other.

Since you left, I haven't gone to the movies anymore. Watching a premiere doesn't bring excitement and enthusiasm like it did in the past. I can't laugh, so there is no point in going to the movies to be solemn and feel detached. I cannot see or connect my thoughts with my vision. My vision has become disconnected from my thoughts. I feel abandoned, and my life lacks meaning. I perceive myself as abandoned, and my life feels devoid of purpose.

Since you have gone, time keeps ticking, yet I find myself trapped in a time warp created by my thoughts. I recall the months before your death. I immersed myself in running the business; I was so busy with the charity planning event after event. Life has changed me. I remember you mentioning problems, and I assumed that you would resolve your issues. I thought you were tough and resilient and could handle life's challenges. I was wrong. You asked for help, and I wasn't there to support you. I kept myself excessively occupied, constantly diverting my attention, which led to feelings of guilt. I was unable to save you from you. I have lived my life, and you have a vibrant future. Since you have gone, I am stagnant, living a life of regret.

Since you have gone, I have continued to live for my remaining children. At eight weeks, I still find it impossible to function. I can't stop thinking about you. I am angry that this has happened. I am depressed, and I don't want to talk with anyone. Life has betrayed me, and everyone has betrayed me. Since you have gone, I have continued to set the table for four people and dish up four meals, only to remember that... The family eats in silence, contrasted with the years of noisy, foolish family chat and banter. The family's togetherness has departed. Since you have gone, we wordlessly fix our gaze upon the now vacant seat that was previously occupied. As the steam rises from the hot food, I forget to eat until it grows cold. After hours of chasing my thoughts and wallowing in sorrow, my mind returned to the table. I look around, and everyone has left. My plate of food has gone cold, and I have yet to eat again.

Since you have gone, I am stuck in a time warp of my thoughts while time continues to tick since you have gone. I recall the months before your death. I immersed myself in running the business; I was so busy with the charity planning event after event. Life has changed me. I remember you mentioning problems, and I assumed that you would resolve your issues. I thought you were tough and resilient and could handle life's challenges. I was wrong. You asked for help, and I wasn't there to support you. I busied myself too much, constantly diverting my attention, which made me feel guilty. I was unable to save you from you. I have lived my life, and you have a vibrant future. Since you have gone, I have been stagnant, living a life of regret....

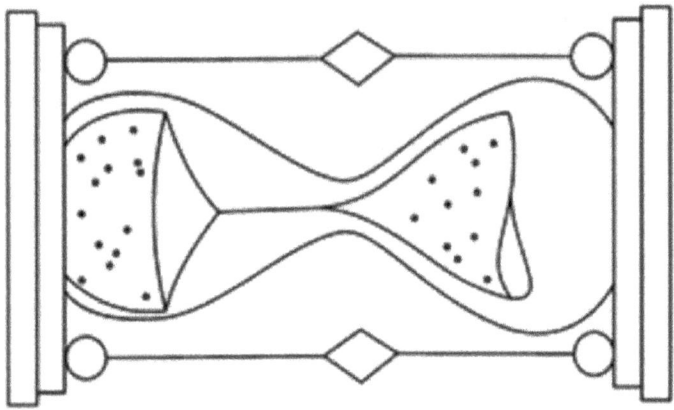

Since you have gone, people and family members have been so judgmental about our loss. We can't get over your death. We need to grieve, and this may take some years. We need to work together as a family to sort our minds to sort out our mixed emotions: anger, sorry, hate, shame, and fear. We need to do things to make us feel like we are living and feel better because we are alive. Parents can join support groups with other families who have gone through the same tragedy so that it will bring greater meaning and purpose to their shattered lives. We need to find good friends and positive family members to talk with. Who we can cry with, who we can share the pain. We need real people who will listen and not be judgmental.

Since you have gone, I have turned to God. I have become religious. I have put my habits of drinking alcohol, swearing, and gambling away. No one can provide me with the answers to my questions. I had two options, and that was to lean on alcohol or to lean on God. I have gained tremendous solace by turning to God. My mind is at ease, and I don't experience the anxiety that I had at the beginning. I have more of a forgiving spirit, and the fear, anger, and bitterness have dissipated. I attend a church down the road and have begun to study the Bible, which I have never understood from an early age. Some issues in life have become more apparent in my direction, and my thoughts are a process. I am on a journey to recovery. I still miss you, but I now have this inner peace. God has filled the void I carried around for so long. I have gained the courage and strength to share my story with others. I have a podcast, and it's about my story. I have over 50,000 followers.

Since you left, we have put your Urn on the middle shelf above the fireplace. We have a large photo of you beside it; the photo was your end-of-year six portrait photo taken at school. Sometimes, in the evening, we sit together and all cry, holding hands and wiping our faces. Words cannot express our emotions and the sad times we experience. Our loss is the most awful event that we can remember in the history of our family. Through the tears through our dark days, we have gathered strength from each other. We vow to continue making good lives for the rest of the siblings. We refer to this as our foundational building stone for our future successes.

Since you have gone, your Dad has worked fewer hours than he used to. He now works part-time. It feels strange when we see him tinkering around the house. We have learned to manage much less money coming in, but we all feel happier together. Having the latest clothes or the latest game consoles doesn't matter anymore. Your sister isn't on social media 24/7 and comes out of her bedroom to converse. We have a more incredible family bond, and those things no longer take precedence. Instead, we give more value to each other as we spend more time together. We often tell each other how much we love each other, which we never used to do. At first, there was awkwardness, but now the warmth is here.

Since you left, I have written my thoughts and hopes for the future in a journal. I bought an excellent journal by Odelyn Smith on Amazon and began writing and documenting the days of surprise and disappointment when I first heard the news. Writing my innermost thoughts, actions, and how my body reacted to the news. The sleepless nights, frequent incontinence, headaches, cold sweats, and dark days that followed the hospital visit to the morgue-were all part of our journey after identifying your body. The feeling of your cold skin contrasted to my heated body. You looked peaceful as I watched you in the room. I saw no chest movements and held my breath, waiting for your breath to return. I write down my thoughts that you are now at rest away from this wicked world. I write about the days of silence when we didn't want to speak and couldn't talk. I write about our permanent separation and how and why you left us. I write about what you were thinking: the cycle of hidden pain and guilt that had been plaguing you. I write about your age, your mind-set, and your temperament. Since you have gone, our role as parents has relinquished, but I continue to write.

Since you have gone, I have taken up a new painting hobby at the local college. I particularly enjoy working with watercolours. I like to mix the paint and water and watch as the elements merge. The bright colours remind me of you and how you would brighten our lives. I enjoy drawing and painting the local scenery of the town where you used to hang out with your friends. I enjoy applying the first strokes of colour onto a blank canvas. The bright colours remind me of a new start, a new beginning. Since you have gone, watercolour painting has become a form of release and relaxation. For a short while, my thoughts have an imaginative focus, but only for a short while.

Since you have gone, we have allowed your siblings to enter your room as part of the healing process. They take care of your collectible teddies. They have placed your action men on the shelf beside your bed. They read your adventure comics together and act out the scenes across the bedroom. Since you have gone, your brother puts on your clothes and will shout, "Get out of my Room!" he sounds more like you every day. I watch them as they play with your Play Station. They have become more respectable and return it to the case as you liked it. Since you have gone, they watch your T.V. for hours. You were choosing to watch the YouTube influencers that you love. They no longer engage in the programs they used to watch. I don't hear them arguing anymore because you are not here. At night, they often fall asleep in your bed. I listen to them crying underneath the covers. Since you have gone...

Since you have gone, we encountered floods of phone calls and text messages. We received cards, email cards, and Facebook notifications from well-wishers. Mum's parenting role became demanding, trying to keep up with the flood of condolences. She had long and detailed telephone conversations with friends and family members. Mum continues to talk with your friends on the phone. Since you have gone, the phone calls used to be daily. Six months later, Mum received phone calls four times a week. A year later, we received one phone call during the week. Mum has been brave.

Since you have gone, I have continued to buy clothes for you at the local store. I bring the clothes home knowing what I have done but not understanding why I have done it. In my heart, I wish that this guilt would disappear and that my fears would dissipate. As I look in the mirror each morning when I shave, I know I can't show you my tips on my perfect shave hacks. When I'm in a better mood, I either return the clothes to the store or donate them to our local charity shop. I usually get around to completing this task during the following week or when I remember. Your absence still shocks me. Since you have gone, I remember your favourite nursery songs. You sang "Humpty Dumpty" all day long when you were three. I remember you falling onto the floor and rolling around, still trying to sing the rest of the song. I can still hear the excitement and your screams of laughter when we rolled around on the fall with you. It was fun, and life was fun then.

Since you have gone, the snooty neighbour next door who never used to talk now says, "Hello." She stopped to chat when she saw us entering the car at the beginning of the school run. Some days, I am politely trying to get away. I can see the sadness in her eyes as she talks and hear her solemn tone of voice. She asks questions but seldom waits for me to answer. The husband smiles and he waves as he goes to work. Sometimes, they will give us a slice of cake from a birthday celebration. This is the neighbour's way of making peace since you have gone.

Since you've been gone, the school has put a plaque inside the school reception area in your remembrance. They had a special ceremony for the unveiling. We were at the ceremony, and so were your close friends. The technology teacher engraved your sports achievements and academic awards. You were such a bright student, a high flyer. Being a high achiever was your legacy; I wish you had lived to continue achieving it.

Since you've been gone, the cat has entered your bedroom at 7:00 am every morning and sits on your bed to meow. The cat was your alarm clock for two years and still proudly performs the duty. The cat waits on your bed until I call him downstairs for breakfast. Since you have gone, he misses your hugs, the pats on the head, the strokes, and the talks you would have with him. Since you have gone, he sits on the window sill, waiting and longing to see your face again.

Since you have gone we have volunteered with the Samaritans in the town.

We have trained to be call handlers and answer phone calls in the evenings. We have learned more about young people and their social struggles in the past year. In local schools, we give talks, share our stories, and raise awareness about death by suicide. We run workshops in the local community during the school holidays. We cover subjects about depression and the well-being of children. In helping others, we have discovered that it helps us through our grief and sorrow. We gain strength in knowing that a young life is safer whenever a child phones, texts, or asks for help.

Since you have gone, the children who used to bully you in school have all left. We heard reports that three families have moved out of the area. We received letters of apologies and cards, often with smudge writing. They have all dispersed like vapour. Since you have gone I remember the afternoon when the two female police officers knocked on the door. I remember the tone of her voice and the look in her eyes as she asked me if she could come in. I remember the smell of the burnt dinner that was on the stove. I remember looking at the clock. I remember the shock and disbelief. I told them that they have the wrong family...

Since you have gone, I have looked through the Family Photograph album to remember the good days. I looked at the photos of you when you were the flower girl at your uncle's wedding. I remember the week before you fell and the nose scar. I look at the photos with the family, especially the scenes of you holding my hand after you had been on the speed boat with your Dad. I saw the photo of you holding my hand as you walked across the bar and balanced at the Adventure Park. Since you have gone, we have continued to exist by submerging ourselves in work and trying not to think about the harrowing past.

Since you have gone, I haven't seen the rainbows, which used to bring me joy when I looked at them. When it rains and the sun shines through, I no longer delight in seeing the prisms of colour. People say, "Time is a healer," but this statement is untrue. I am in a cycle of actions dictated by my mood, and I struggle to get into a routine. Since you have gone, years have passed, and I still blame myself for your death. I go for long walks by the canal and in the woods. I have no delight when autumn arrives, and the leaves fall from the trees. Why wasn't I more alert? Why didn't I see the signs? The bottom line is that I had failed as a parent.

Since you have gone, the well-kept vegetable patch in the garden has become overgrown with weeds. The un-harvested carrots and beetroots grow rotten and brown. The garden used to be our daily project that you would attend to. We aimed to cultivate another square meter of a different type of vegetable each year. I remember you spending hours on weeding and then tilling the ground. I remember the bottles of water that you drank on that day. I saw your determination to finish the task. Since you have gone, we need the will or the motivation to continue with the vegetable patch. Sometimes, we sit in the overgrown garden to think about how life has changed.

Notes

Plan of action

9

Comfort

This chapter will attempt to show how a relationship gap can widen. Various scenarios will show how distance can cause division and misunderstanding. The distance I write about in this chapter is not referring to physical distance. The distance is a widening gap that seeks to destroy a friendship. The friend may be looking for ways in which to rebuild their friendship. The widening gap is a mixture of tension, fear, and insecurity. Resolution of the problems is the key; the friendship can resume once they disappear.

This chapter will show the mis/under-rated social society that young people affiliate to. The gap is the relationship between the parents and their child. Vital components of youth society are the online networking friendship communities. This friendship is crucial/essential/indispensable. It is like explaining the football offside rule: either you understand it, or you don't. (I still don't understand it). The misunderstandings and the missing links are often unknown to parents. Parents need to foster knowledge of youth society and plan ways of rebuilding trust and value.

The Close Friend

You have heard your best friend say the odd comments about their life. One comment made you stop and think. The conversation continued, and the subject changed...... but you were uncomfortable about the comment. Your friend was fun, always chatty, and had a brilliant sense of humour. You have enjoyed playing off each other for years, saying bad jokes, and sharing toys. You often eat lunch together and exchange sweets, but this has changed.

Now, a change in their character has occurred. The once brave, fearless friend has become the worried recluse. As a close friend, you have spoken about the problem and given advice. You have suggested so many ways to resolve the issues. Your friend has listened to your guidance and has taken things on board. The situation has not changed, and your friend looks worse. As a friend, you can choose to stand there helpless, looking on, not knowing what the outcome will be. Or you can opt to share the problem with a trusted parent or a school teacher.

Why is this happening? You sit and wonder and are now worried about your friend's well-being. Your friend needs to become more active in their communication. Their stare often mars the engagement in conversation. The regular three-weekly meet-up has now converted into a monthly advice session. There's no fun, no play, but boring repetition conversation. Your friendship has changed, but you don't understand why. And the how? The dynamics have shifted, and you don't know how to reset. You know you can help, but everything you have said and done recently has failed. You can see both the pain and the fear on your friend's face.

You are now on a secret mission of getting external help. You are planning the best strategy for this delicate situation. At the beginning of the year, you had made censorship promises to each other. In your heart, you believe that the impending dome of death by suicide is looming on the horizon. You want to put this all to the back of your mind, but you can't. The talk of death is a "release," and "no one cares," and the "I want to die talk" is scary. You want to say something to an adult but have sworn to secrecy. Your allegiance between a friendship and doing what is right for your friend is the battle. You have tried to resolve the situation for six months, and nothing has changed. Now it's time to get help from an adult. It's time to talk.

If you feel more comfortable approaching your parents, then do so. Confide in your parents, a teacher, or a responsible adult. Your friend may choose to ostracise you. Or even a decline in communication, which may change the flow of your friendship for a short while. Your friend may say that you

COMFORT

have betrayed your friendship. Rest assured that your decision to share the information is the best. Please do not feel guilty and understand that you have opened a door of help for them. The opportunity to access help and restoration is a process that takes time. Your friend may need to access a range of services from health professionals.

It is a challenging task to resolve deep-rooted problems of your own. It is a more difficult task to fix the issues that your adolescent friend is having. The first step is to tell a responsible adult about your friend's problems. The adult will ask for support and guidance from a health professional. The final phase is when the young person accesses the resources to resolve their problems. After disclosing the adolescent's problems, actions for change can begin. Be comforted that you have chosen the right option for the health and well-being of your friend. Do not feel guilty or downtrodden about your decision. Think of it as you have given your friend a get-out-of-jail-free card in Monopoly. Believe and have faith that your friendship will return to normal in the future. Stay positive in your mind and stay true to your friend. Stay positive in your mind and remain true to your friend. Affirm with your friend every time that you meet; this will help them in the healing process.

Be comforted that you have done the right thing. You have taken positive steps in resolving something that you couldn't fix. Keep focused on your friend, think of the things that would bring them joy, and do it. Think of fun and exciting things to do and plan to do them. Go to a theme park, go fishing or to a skate park, watch a movie, or have a pizza night.

The Young Person

Some teens will experiment with alcohol and engage on a slippery slope to destruction. At the same time, other young people start on the additive path of narcotics. For a split moment, conjoined thoughts and blissful peace numb the pain of life. They no longer feel the pain; their mind has lost focus. Temporary releases do not provide permanent solutions to inner pain. Peace is a fulfillment of you, and like the missing piece of the jigsaw puzzle, it will complete you. The pursuit of peace can be a lifelong ambition for some people. Peace is a pursuit; it's like chasing something you need, and peace is running away from you. You have to achieve peace and feel complete; you have to be at peace to continue your life.

Young people and teens must become receptive to change. (Article the 5 R's) They must gain strength and resilience in something in someone to build them back up. Both physical and mental restoration must take place.

The Parent

Parents may read this book because they need a solution to their teen problem. As a parent, you may be at your wit's end. Something is wrong with their child, and their behaviour has changed. Their patterns of communication have changed. You see that the change is not for good, and you have seen a decline in their habits and behaviour. You have tried to find out why, but you are not satisfied with the answers given. You have attempted to question their best friend. You are even more frustrated by their youthful tight-lipped. As a parent, you have begun to question the validity of your parental role. You have now started to worry about your child's health, mental health, and well-being. Again, you try to ask their friends questions, but it's a close-knit community of thinkers. However, they deny and say that everything is ok. In your heart, you know that there is something drastically wrong.

You have a parental hunch that something is wrong, and you experience a numbness that is eating you away. Parents need to work out how to approach their child. You must muster up the courage to ask the question, "Are you thinking of taking your life?" If the answer is no, continue to watch and deliberate whether this was an answer to throw you off the scent. There may be underlying issues that need sorting out, so be on your guard. Interact as much as possible with your child or adolescent. Have conversations and do household chores together. Be in their space where they like to do things. Linger in the areas of the home where your child usually hangs out. Become cooler than usual and sound more trendy by using their slang. Offer to buy new items for their bedroom as an excuse to gain access to probe the area.

As a parent, the ideal for your child is to have a "Happy and Prosperous Life." To consider death by suicide was not an option; it is quite a shock when you hear those words. You feel all sorts of mixed emotions. You're in a state of denial. Parents need to keep their thoughts together and use their energy to plan for their future. Don't let fear cloud your mind. Reach out to give more support and reassurance to your child first. Tell them that together, you can go through their difficulties. As a parent, you must put your life on hold and free up some time. Engage in conversations and plan activities together. If you both like to walk and talk, then do so. If you enjoy washing the dishes together, then do it. Whatever you feel comfortable doing together, could you do it? Don't procrastinate! Don't become a defeatist!

Don't pretend it is a phase that will blow over. Don't be ignorant and lazy in your approach. Stay positive; through this problematic phase, there will be a breakthrough. Develop resilience and go forward armed with a plan of action.

As a parent, you have had awkward conversations with your child. You have asked an important question. Are you thinking of death by suicide? And the response is, "Yes." You may feel shocked and need a short time to recover. Muster your strength together. Be clear about your direction, and write down the strategy. Your heart is heavy with the news, but you must continue to look like a robust and supportive parent. The fact that your child has divulged the matter to you is a good starting point. You are in a position to help your child.

They have contacted you, and now you need to connect them to the support they need. Communicate daily and, importantly, follow through with your plan of action.

Your next steps will be to ask your child questions and write down as much information as possible. Write down the data after you have had conversations. Use the listening skills that you have acquired and keep strong.

Decide on the course of action. Take action!

Contact the relevant support agencies. Ask whether they can assist you with a young person who is considering death by suicide. Arrange a face-to-face meeting with a teacher from the child's school. The information must be strictly confidential and not disclosed to the students under any circumstances. Please ensure that complete confidentiality is maintained.

Establish a method of communication that you are comfortable with. You should contact the teacher by telephone or by email. Update the teacher with progress every week. Keep the young person or adolescent informed about what is going on. Include adolescents in the decision-making by giving options. As a parent, you can inform your child about all or some agencies you are contacting. Assess their well-being and decide on when and what to divulge. Remember, they are very fragile, trying to cope with their situation. As a parent, continue to show your physical support. Give regular hugs or gentle pats on the back to reassure them that you are there. Cook their favourite meals and speak positive words. Watch the television together but avoid watching the news. The news is a mixture of negative doom and gloom; stay away from it. If your child enjoys gaming, encourage them to continue. At least one hour before bed, ask them to stop so that they can have a better night's sleep. The problems may take months to understand. Be patient and dedicate your time to learning and understanding. Be sympathetic in every way you can, and use a journal to document your thoughts. Build on your relationship and investigate how you can get closer to your child.

Parent emotions are essential, too. The best way that you can be the best parent is to apply a good dose of self-care. Listen to soothing music in the car when you are driving. Listen to this incredible, soft music before you go to bed. Relaxing music enables you to unwind and think more. Speak with close family members and friends. Only seek to have conversations with those who will uplift and encourage you. Reject all types of negative conversations. Affirm daily and whenever you can, take time for self-care. Remember, you are not the only parent, friend, or guardian going through this.

The problems may take months to understand. Be patient and dedicate time to learning and understanding your child's problems. Be sympathetic in every way you can, and use a journal to document your thoughts. Build on your relationship and investigate how you can get closer to your child. Parent emotions are essential, too. The best way that you can be the best parent is to apply a good dose of self-care. Listen to soothing music in the car when you are driving. Listen to this incredible, soft music before you go to bed. Relaxing music enables you to unwind and think more. Speak with close family members and friends. Only seek to have conversations with those who will uplift and encourage you. Reject all types of negative conversations. Affirm daily and whenever you can, take time for self-care. Remember, you are not the only parent, friend, or guardian going through this.

Notes

Plan of action

10

FAQ Youth Suicide Prevention

This chapter aims to address any missed or misunderstood aspects of learning that occurred while reading the book, seeking to fill in those gaps comprehensively. The FAQ section is a prompt and a guide to steer parents in the correct direction that would answer their questions. It will provide concentrated, quick solutions to young people's problems. It offers fast and easy access to valuable answers about youth suicide prevention. It's a quick reference and guide. The FAQ chapter is a brilliant source of content. The chapter will help me to understand and serve the book-reading audience better.

Q: When is the best time to talk and discuss with my child?

A: This will depend on the young person's willingness to converse. The main focus is to grapple with enough time to have a conversation. From that small conversation, the next time, it will be a lot longer until you achieve the status of having an in-depth discussion without interruptions. The information will lead to resolution and restoration of the whole body and mind. As a parent, you will need to plan many conversations—plan to have a conversation during the morning run-of-the-mill routines. Conforming in the evening after school or before bed at night is possible. Whenever you feel that the time is right, ask the questions. The communication may be pretty pleasant until the Inquisition begins. Remember, the atmosphere may change. The subject matter will be the cause for the solemn atmosphere change. Keep talking, and continue gathering as much information as you can hear.

Q: How can I converse with my child about their emotions? What should I do?

A: You can approach the young person with a bit of humour. This element of humour at the beginning of the conversation will break the ice. The humour can be a focus on an item in the room. Or it can be an experience you can share that will bring laughter. In no way should the humour be a focus on the child. If it is, that would make them sad and more insecure. The purpose of the humour is to set them at ease. As a parent, you create a laidback, informal, approachable atmosphere. Begin the conversation by being relational. Share a situation where, in your younger years, you had found it challenging to communicate. Your purpose is to gain their confidence and trust by sharing your experience. The adolescent will prepare for their time of sharing. They will have time to order their emotions and respond to the questions.

Q: Where is the ideal place to have a conversation with my child about death by suicide?

A: You can speak with your child in a variety of locations. You can talk to your child when you are at home. You can relax together in the living room, watching the TV and starting a conversation there. You can speak to your child while traveling in the car before or after school. You can create a conversation there but may not have the time to complete it. Dinner time is another ideal setting where you can converse while eating. You may be an active family who enjoys taking an evening stroll. The evening stroll is an opportune time to initiate a discussion about suicide. The ideal place you have in your mind may not be where you have this conversation. As a parent, become an opportunist and ask the question. This task is highly challenging, but being asked to do it signifies overcoming the initial hurdle.

Q: As a parent of teenagers, I am concerned about the mental well-being of my child's best friend. Should I speak with the young person about their problems?

A: If you have an excellent communicative relationship with the young person, the answer is "Yes." It would help you to understand what the problem may be. Having a good rapport with the young person helps in this situation. Tell the adolescent you cannot keep what they tell you a secret. After your discussion, write down as much information as possible.

Q: Should I tell the parents of the teen about their child's problems?

A: Yes, you should. If you know the parents very well, arrange to meet to discuss your concerns. Ask that the young person is absent during this meeting. Your position is to inform and alert the child's parents about your concerns and their problems. Discuss what you have observed, what you have heard from other peers, and what you have spoken about. Request a face-to-face meeting and state that it is of great importance. Meet with the parents at the quickest possible time.

Q: What method of communication should I use to contact the adolescent parents?

A: There are many methods that you can use to arrange for a meeting. The choice ultimately relies on what makes you most comfortable. You can choose to call the parents if you know their telephone number. If you feel confident, then call them via video call. Another method of communication is to send an email. If you feel confident, then contact them via video call. Another method of communication is to send an email. In the email, introduce yourself. Request a face-to-face meeting so that you can discuss some concerns that you have for their child. Do not mention "death by suicide" in your email; this information will be too distressing. The email is not to alarm the parents, but instead, it is to inform gently. Leave the detailed points for the face-to-face meeting. Approach the email from an informal standpoint. Use words and phrases such as "gentle," "work together," and "young people's perspective of life." These phrases will reduce the trauma and distress for the parents. Flag the email as urgent so that the recipient reads it immediately. Leave your mobile phone number as a method of communication. The parents may want to contact you to verify that you are a human and that the email is not spam.

You can choose to send a high-priority message in WhatsApp. You can send an Android text message and mark it as urgent. You can do this by typing your text message on the phone. Instead of tapping the send button, hold it, and it should give you a box labelled "urgent." If you are still waiting for a response within 24 hours, send a different communication form.

The last but efficient method would be to go to their home and organise a meeting. Request a face-to-face meeting as soon as possible. Remember to ask that the teen be absent during the initial meeting. Post a handwritten note through their front door if no one is home. Remember to put a contact telephone number as a method of communication. As a concerned parent, you would have taken the necessary steps to offer support and care.

Before meeting with the parent, record the essential facts. What you have observed is the discussions that you have had with your child about their friend. Prepare the notes that you have written after your conversation with the adolescent. Compile your thoughts and suggestions for help. Condense and review all your ideas and reflections. Identify the triggers and the problems that you have identified. Together, you can all plan resolutions to the issues discussed. Work with the parents to create a plan of action. Discuss the type of professional agencies and the needed support methods. Before leaving the meeting, set a date and a time for the next session.

Q: As a parent, should I approach a medical specialist to help my child?

A: Yes, if you are very worried and are sure this is the route that will help. Please book an appointment with your local doctor and explain to your child that they must be present. Bring your notes and refer to them during the appointment. The doctor will ask you and your child questions. Your doctor may refer your child to see a more specialist health professional. This person may be in the field of child psychiatry, especially if there's a history of anxiety or stress. The doctor may make a referral to a specialist in the area of young people's nutrition and well-being. Having the added support and input from health professionals is reassuring. Support may be the key to the much-needed help that the teen may need at that particular moment.

Q: Should I talk with my child about death by suicide when they have their friends in our home?

A: No, this is not the correct way of obtaining your desired responses. If the young person has friends in your home, this is not the ideal time for this conversation. Your child's focus will be on chillaxing and enjoying their company. If your child is rushing out of the home to see a friend, then that is not the ideal time to stop and request a conversation. Selecting time to communicate with your child can be difficult, but it is vital. Young people play the avoidance game, so scheduling a time to talk becomes quite a task. Choose a specific date and time when you can set a definitive appointment. Give your child time to respond. Become more understanding in your approach. Reassure your child by affirming them. You can use the following phrases:

"You are worthy of love and respect right now."

"You are resilient and can bounce back from setbacks."

"You are surrounded by people who support and care about you."

"I believe in you and your ability to overcome challenges." And you can say, "You are resilient and can bounce back from setbacks."

Q: Is it necessary to be in a secluded and confined area to talk about suicide?

A: Yes, a quiet place where you can talk is ideal. The environment should be calm and chilled, so there's no added pressure to listen. It would help if you didn't go to a place with loud music playing. Communication will take a lot of work. Vital information can be lost in translation or misunderstood. The parent and the young person can become frustrated when the background music is too loud. The background music should be soft, soothing, and tranquil.

Q: Is it advisable for me to embrace the responsibility of listening to a child's or young person's concerns?

A: This is entirely your choice. In the first instance, you may not want the responsibility of listening to a young person's concerns. In your mind, you may feel as though you are strong enough to cope with the answer to the over-arching question. "Are you thinking of taking your life by suicide?" If the answer is "Yes," then you are unsure how to cope with that outcome. You can make a referral to a suitable professional person or organisation. These people would be able to assess and assist the young person.

But, if the answer was "No," you could cope with the responsibility of listening to their concerns. Children and adolescents face various problems, so confiding in an adult is crucial. Embracing the burden of listening is very rewarding. Your future supportive steps will enable the young person to become the champion.

Q: What strategies can I use to cope after a disclosure?

A: Some parents may be unable to cope with the details of what they hear. The information may need to be more manageable. The shock and the heartbreak can cause anxiety and depression. Some parents may feel inadequate and helpless in their approach. They know they must help their child, but the how and the understanding are challenging. Some parents may adapt their working life to focus on their child's well-being. Spend the time listening and showing empathy. Ask lots of questions and come to a good understanding of the problems. Take appropriate action and begin the process of change. Knowing and coping with the truth takes work. Surround yourself with a supportive network of friends and family members. Remember that the mental well-being of both the adolescent and the parent is imperative. Contact charitable agencies and organisations that can provide advice. Kindly review the information on the back pages of this book for further help.

Q: Should I inform the young person's school that they want to take their life?

A: As a parent, this would be a wise precaution. Request a face-to-face meeting with the school principal. Ask for the academic head of the year to attend the meeting. They can assist with your child's educational intervention program. Ask for the form teacher to attend. They can provide valuable insight into the classroom dynamics. Consider inviting other school health professionals. In an ideal world, all the school staff would be in attendance to make the decision process quicker. To ensure an accurate record, have the meeting minutes written down. Finally, come up with a plan on how to fix the problems the child is facing.

Q: Are you experiencing any issues or concerns due to the information shared?

A: You might have a hunch or a gut feeling, making you fear the information you receive. Your gut feeling may affect future death-by-suicide conversations. As a parent, you may also be grappling with the issue of death by suicide. Your low self-esteem is the mirror image that your child reflects. If this is the case, you should seek help for yourself and your child. Stay positive and think positive. Create a plan of action and write down your thoughts and feelings. Speak with a supportive family member or a close friend who can offer you help during this time. Contact your doctor or other health professionals who assess and assist you. They can give you a medical evaluation and establish the appropriate support systems.

Q: Why is it so important to take notes?

A: Note-taking is a quick and easy way of recording information. Note-taking can take place during or shortly after the event. Note-taking is the summarising of vast amounts of data. You are more likely to remember and to recall situations after the process of note-taking. Note-taking engages your mind to re-organize, process, and store by writing. Note-taking is the recording of vital data that will help you in the future. After the conversations that you have with your child, note-taking is essential. Note-taking is essential during the meetings with the principal and other school personnel. Listen carefully and be consistent in your note-taking. After each meeting, read your notes, and then refine the sentences. Add more pieces of data. Omit sections that are not relevant. Write your next steps. Put the meeting documents in a folder in chronological order. Your notes will reference when you need to recall the information. During future meetings, your detailed notes will help you to communicate your points.

Q: Why is note-taking important?

A: Note-taking is essential because you develop a deeper understanding of the subject. You are summarising large pieces of information into bite-sized pieces. Good note-taking serves as a reference for future meetings. People typically estimate that they will retain around 30% of the information discussed in meetings. Note-taking is a helpful prompt for the mind to regurgitate text. Good note-taking is a starting point for a report that a parent can write about a trigger or an incident. Effective note-taking shows the various strategies of change that parents can focus on.

Q: How can I make notes?

A: There are various methods for taking notes, so choose the method which is most suited for you. The outline method of note-taking summarises your notes into main topics and sub-topics. This method is handy when you need to review specific points.

Short-hand note-taking is the abbreviation of words, phrases, and symbols. The short-hand method is suitable for recording information quickly. When there are many people in a meeting, the exchange of information is quick. The short-hand method is more convenient.

Bullet point notation is an excellent method. Dots or dashes followed by short, concise sentences make it easy to present details.

Mind mapping is a handy method of using diagrams to replicate information. If this is your preferred note-taking method, please bring lots of paper. You can combine mind mapping with any of the other mentioned methods. Highlight the sentences that will provide opportunities for future meetings.

Q: How effective is note-taking in this situation?

A: Yes, notes can help the young person in need. Your notes will serve as your diary, where you will log your thoughts. Notes can help you write an incident log. Keeping a diary is your record of the events that occur chronologically. It's a valuable tool for recognizing the triggers and events your child has encountered. What your child has experienced and what you have seen and understood are very important. Your diary is a comprehensive timeline of events. Adapt the sentences to fit various situations that you would like to address. Good note-taking leads to good preparation. Effective note-taking will provide answers for the next steps.

Q: Why is a plan of action necessary?

A: Parents should create a plan of action for their child. An action plan aims to identify the resources the parent needs to reach their goal. The plan of action is necessary to establish individual or joint family goals. It provides a clear and organised path for you to follow. The resources and support agencies are necessary for the change process. Close family members and friends will come to a more excellent knowledge of the plan of action. As a team, you can all work towards achieving your objectives. They can all get involved in the healing process. The action plan will adhere to the goals by scheduling and prioritizing tasks. Adapt small achievable goals and tasks that will take a little effort. The plan of action is a framework for success, so the grey areas of uncertainty will disappear. The action plan is necessary because it is measurable and allows for tracking. A plan of action helps parents to align support with the ideals for their child's well-being. The plan of action is an avenue to start communication and engagement. It provides a structured approach to the issues that your child is facing.

Q: What elements should a parent include in their plan of action?

A: The plan of action should be simple step-by-step instructions on how to achieve each of your parental goals. Your plan of action may be a variety of goals. The elements included are a detailed catalogue of events and possible resolutions. The elements will also include detailed notes from meetings with school personnel. The plan of action will include your thoughts and feelings. Instead, the open forum will provide a platform for the parent and adolescent to talk. Your action plan will provide a clear, organised pathway for achieving your goals. Work towards achieving your goal before the next meeting with the school officials. Work towards putting the health support in place before the next meeting. Work towards a schedule to achieve your goals for the plan of action. Work on your plan of action every day. Prioritise your workload and be purposeful in your choice of tasks. Let the mundane daily home tasks wait for a while. Your more important goal is that you are happy in your pathway of success for your child's well-being. Scheduled appointments with the young person are necessary at this point. Your appointments will be time to discuss your action plan and keep your child informed. Answer all the questions that your child may have and discuss any fears that they may have. As a parent, you will become more susceptible to their needs and support strategies.

Q: How should I prepare my child to attend a meeting?

A: It's essential to communicate the meeting date to the young person. Do not hide the meeting details from them. Name the school officials and the health professionals who will be there. Discuss the topics on the agenda for the discussion. Answer all questions that the young person may have. Be honest with your answers, and don't gloss over the facts. The young person needs time to digest the information. Ask the young person different questions so that they can prepare their answers before the meeting. The questions will let the young person get in tune with their emotions and think about how to answer. Don't allow your child to attend this important meeting with a friend. Attending the meetings together is highly beneficial for parents and their children. As a concerned parent, your focus is to bridge the gap and to reach their troubled mind. When the young person attends the first meeting, it is an outstanding achievement. The young person is acknowledging that they need external help. The young person is reaching out to you, so try to gain their trust and confidence.

Q: Who should I tell about the plan of action?

A: As a parent, you can inform close family members and friends about the circumstances. Select elements of the plan of action that you want to share. Close family members and friends can provide emotional support and encouragement. Please choose whether you want them to speak with your child. They will develop a deeper understanding of suicide prevention. As they become more informed about the situation then you can discuss more about the facts. They could even provide some answers to missing pieces of unknown information. Close family members and friends will now become the watch people. They are well-informed if you need to take a break or have to attend a meeting alone. They all have a part to play in the plan of action. Remember, the English proverbial "A problem shared is a problem halved" is such a true saying in this circumstance of suicide prevention. Don't keep this all to yourself. Don't think it is uncomfortable and that others should not know. Stay positive and focused.

Share elements of the plan of action with any close friends that your child has and with other siblings. Choose the level of intimacy that you would like to disclose. The young person might be open to sharing information that hasn't been disclosed before. Update your plan of action as the events unfold.

Q: How can I communicate the fact that my child is contemplating suicide to siblings?

A: Communicating details about this sensitive topic is not easy. As a parent, you can approach it from different perspectives. If siblings are too young to understand death and suicide, then be precautious. There are several approaches that you can take. Have an awareness discussion about emotions and feelings. Parents can play YouTube videos about the subject and discuss the themes. Younger siblings will gain an insight into their emotions and feelings. By conducting this mini-workshop, they will look at their sibling's actions. Some may even start to report incidents hidden from you in the past. Some siblings are old enough to understand but don't have the maturity. In this case, I would err on the side of caution. Select how much information you will share and your method of sharing. If siblings are old enough to understand, they will offer support during the journey. Parents know the characters of their children. Some children are natural worriers, while others are carefree. Some children are mature, while others are immature. Whatever the case, remember to approach it with caution and sensitivity. Your parental mission is to prevent future episodes of distress propagated by siblings. You are creating an environment of self-awareness and support. Write down important details that you discover during this time of mindfulness.

SUICIDE AWARENESS AND PREVENTION

Q: If my friend is considering death by suicide, is it appropriate for me to tell someone?

A: If your friend is considering death by suicide, yes, it is appropriate to tell someone. Please consider the possible outcome if you decide not to say anything. Consider how you will feel knowing that you kept this information secret and could have changed their future. Approach an adult that you are comfortable speaking to. The adult can be a teacher in your school, an adult at your youth club, or you can confide in your parents. You may have promised not to tell anyone about your private talks. You must break your promise to them and speak to an adult on this occasion. Your friend needs professional help, so by informing an adult, you are helping your friend. You may feel like a traitor; your friend may call you names and refuse to speak. The young person's actions are pretty normal behaviour, given the circumstances. Remember that this behaviour is only for a short time, and rest assured that you are doing the right thing.

Q: When you know that a young person is considering death by suicide, what should you do next?

A: Several factors require consideration. As a parent, your next step would be to contact the relevant support agencies. The first port of call would be to speak with your local doctor. If you're an apprehensive adult who has been made aware of a young person's intentions, please contact the young person's parents or guardians. If you are a family member, don't hesitate to contact the young person's parents. Never tell a young person that you will keep this information secret. Always disclose the information to their parents or a health professional as quickly as possible because your actions will help them in the future. Exposing the truth will change their future, and it potentially helps to keep them alive.

Q: Have you been experiencing suicidal thoughts as a parent?

A: If you're experiencing suicidal thoughts, it is crucial to seek medical assistance and support for both yourself and your child. Don't delay seeking help this should be done immediately. Consider reaching out to a trusted friend or family member for external support. At this point in your journey you may need someone to talk to and to share your thoughts. If that's not feasible, contact a charitable organisation to speak confidentially about your feelings. Make arrangements for a follow-up appointment after taking these initial steps to ensure on-going support and guidance. Health professionals, such as psychiatrists, psychologists, or primary care physicians, can assess the severity and type of condition that you are experiencing. They use various methods, including interviews, questionnaires, and observations, to diagnose your condition accurately. Based on the assessment, health professionals can develop a personalised treatment plan. This may include therapy, medication, lifestyle changes, or a combination of these approaches. Lifestyle modifications will include regular exercise, healthy eating, stress reduction techniques, and improving sleep patterns, as these can significantly impact mood and overall well-being. Remember that you are not alone and there is always someone who is willing to listen and help.

Notes

Plan of action

11

Conclusion

Does a young person need your help?

We live in a society that counts the sad statistics of its youth. The author penned this book to help and guide bewildered, worried parents. The theme of the book was to provide a starting point with essential insights into youth suicide prevention methods. Through the complicated maze of hormones and uncertainty, the book explored the many questions and answers. It addressed some of the stigmatic questions associated with death by suicide. Our youth society of AI is swift and has brought many changes. Young people have more gadgets to help in their day-to-day living, but there is still a lack of vital family time. The importance of addressing youth death by suicide is crucial for their existence, the strategies, and how they might affect families, schools, and communities.

The strategies outlined in the book are significant in the prevention of death by suicide. The book outlines to parents that spending more time with their children will provide more of a cushion for them against the wiles of the society that they live in. With faster-paced adults chasing work demands, there is no time for stopping and analysing life. This book pulls together the key questions and phrases that parents can use to keep an observational eye on their children. This book is relational because our circumstances dictate how we work and live. Economically, if parents' outgoings are higher than their incomings, they will naturally juggle with the means they have left.

The key strategies for the book are helping parents to identify signs of separation and loneliness that can lead to depression. The book will help parents spot a decline in the mood or actions of their child and quickly understand their reason. The book also aims to assist parents in recognizing aspects of their lives that require adjustment or transformation. The book is an essential tool in the fight for the health and well-being of children. The book suggests ways to shape children's eating habits by modelling social interaction with food. This book guides parents, concerned family members, and other adults with the same concerns. The book is easy to read and understand, providing straightforward navigation for its readers. You can read the book repeatedly and write personal notes in the plan of action and notes sections at the end of each Chapter. As an intervention method, the book is a valuable starting point for a general medical assessment or a mental health report.

The critical approaches discussed throughout the book are the repeated phrases and the questions that form the Chapter. The phrase "I need to tell you something" is declarative. This phrase provides the foundation for conversations posed in Chapter 1. As a sentence starter, it has reassuring elements that act as a bandage over a fresh wound. Each sentence is positive. Parents can select relevant sentences and phrases to use. The sentences defuse a trigger or a situation before it escalates. Each positive phrase motivates and empowers parents as they tread the winding paths of emotions. For the reader, the sentences provide an in-depth understanding of adolescent life. These sentences speak life and value; it is the medicine that the young person needs.

The theme for Chapter 2 revolved around fostering a supportive environment. The focus was on emotions, mental states, and understanding one's feelings. "How do you feel?" was the main question, which was simple but effective. In our fast-paced society, we rush to get ready for work. We run to work, and then we rush to go home from work. Life has become more complex through tasks, bills, and a demanding boss. We must actively monitor the well-being of our children in our treadmill lifestyle. For many of us, the office has entered our homes. As parents, we work our regular 9-5 hours. Then, we work overtime hours and dedicate a menial part of our evening to family life. This Chapter contains numerous questions that can boost the mental well-being of young people. Parents can use the questions to determine what is needed to understand the areas of life their child finds difficult to manage. This Chapter is essential because children and young people should get to understand their feelings and know how to deflect their course of action.

With a clear emphasis on remembering a happy past, Chapter 3 is thought-provoking. Happy memories are usually attached to an event or something that we cherish. When recalled from the happy archive, our brain comprises sentences with merry sentiments connected. "You were happy when" is a reminiscence of the good old days. Their family environment felt the emotional connection, joy, contentment, and bliss. These phrases and sentences are a pleasant trip down memory lane, which will bring reassurance and a longing for the feelings they felt at that time. The flashbacks and the reflections are a catalogue of events the young person will enjoy. The phrase "You were happy when" forms a sense of belonging and love instead of isolation and loneliness. These critical approaches discussed throughout Chapter 3 reference the happy things in life. Parents will have a clearer understanding of youthful happiness.

Throughout Chapter 4, a consistent emphasis was evident regarding the thought-provoking question, "Are you happy with you?" Under a variety of categories, well-being is the knowledge of being healthy. It's a direct question to a child or young person about their happiness. It is an individualistic question that only the young person can answer truthfully. In Chapter 4, the questions reveal the layers of joy a young person may feel. The questions will help to decipher their inner thoughts and how they will allude to happiness. Parents will be able to identify whether their child knows they are happy. As parents, it is evident that well-being is not tangible.

The "Are you happy with you?" questions will help as a layer to understand happiness levels. The questions will aid in rediscovering how to express happiness. Parents and their children can demonstrate happiness in various ways. The questions will guide you towards experiencing episodes of happiness by describing them as good memories. The questions will lead to episodes of joy. By looking at the happiness in the home, parents can see the reflection of the happiness that the young person will eventually show. It will change the way people speak about happiness. This Chapter has made parents more aware of the layers and the different stages of happiness. One can create happiness, but inner happiness must stem from within oneself. The range of questions relating to the "Are you happy with you?" is a good starting point for bewildered parents. Over time, parents will make sense of the chaotic situations that they are in.

Chapter 5 emphasized the questions squarely, commencing with the words "Can we?" It is a simple question to inquire about the possibility or ability to do something. The word "can is a modal verb of ability; it's a prompting word, leading and requiring an action." (Oxford University Press, 2023, p.)

The word "we" in the question isn't solely about individual participation but rather about cultivating togetherness and joint involvement. The response to these questions can either be positive or negative. The young person can choose to respond positively by taking part in the activity or action required. "Can we?" are questions used to challenge the feasibility of doing something. Parents can use the questions as a critical strategy or adapt and create their own. The "Can we?" questions can use covert analysis to determine through their actions whether they are open to change. The "Can we?" questions act as a filter revealing the mind-set of the adolescent. Someone is leading the young person into accepting one of the invitations. The young person starts to engage through agreement, a positive response.

Chapter 6 placed significant emphasis on the importance of early intervention strategies. The statement "I need to ask you something" is used by parents to initiate a discussion. Parents could start a conversation about a specific subject, which will lead to more questions that will reveal the thought patterns of the young person. Parents may ask the statement because they are sharing their concerns with their child. Parents will require information and clarification on matters they want to address. Misunderstandings occur often within teenaged households. "I need to ask you something?" is a brilliant way of addressing misunderstanding. Throughout the journey, parents are constantly seeking information. The questions for this Chapter will provide the answers that will help them in their quest for the recovery and restoration of their child. Parents and friends reading this Chapter should be mindful that the child may not be willing to share information at first. As time goes on, their actions and reactions will change. As discussed in the Chapter, parents must initiate changes for endorsement by the journey's end. Chapter 6 encourages parents to develop communication and listening skills to achieve their goals.

"Since you have gone" Chapter 7 was quite a problematic Chapter to write. The Chapter is futuristic and depicts events that could transpire. This Chapter is an attempt to show the lives of family members and friends should death by suicide occur. This Chapter educates the readers about the repercussions of a sudden death on a family. Having a sudden death in a family is not easy to finance. Financing a funeral can lead to a rapid decline in money and increased debt due to borrowing. The phrase "Since you have gone" shows the mental repercussions. This Chapter shows how the experiences and emotions leading up to the sudden death can impact a parent's well-being. The impact on health and the thoughts of the mind may lead to depression and depreciated health. What might transpire will be the professional counselling and the frequency of medical appointments? "Since You Have Gone" examines family relationships and how the atmosphere between parents and siblings can become more strained in the home. This Chapter outlines the various negative and positive outcomes of this situation. This Chapter portrays both the adverse and beneficial consequences stemming from youth death by suicide.

"Comfort" is the title given to Chapter 8. This Chapter showed how collaborative actions can reduce a gap in understanding between parents and adolescents. It is crucial to acknowledge that each young person copes differently. Various situations in life will show how distance can cause division and misunderstanding. The distance does not refer to a physical distance but to parent-child relationships. The distances are the misunderstanding that exists between adults and adolescents. A lack of understanding can destroy a relationship. Parents need to foster knowledge of youth society and plan ways of rebuilding trust and value. This Chapter explores the under-rated social society that young people affiliate to. The friend may be looking for ways in which to rebuild their friendship. The widening gap is the growing tension, fear, and insecurity both parties may feel. Resolution of the problems is the key; once the problems disappear, friendships can resume.

The approach for Chapter 9 was a summary of the "Frequently asked questions about youth suicide prevention" the rationale explained. This Chapter is a brilliant source of information. The questions and answers will guide parents toward answering their questions. This Chapter will bring clarity and accessible knowledge that parents can use readily. The questions and answers will equip and educate parents so that they can avoid the pitfalls along their journey. Chapter 9 presents immediate answers to commonly asked questions without requiring direct inquiry.

Taking action can save a life with these time-saving questions. For young people, the questions and answers will provide concentrated, quick solutions to their problems. The Chapter offers quick and easy access to valuable answers about youth suicide prevention.

CONCLUSION

The critical approaches discussed throughout the book

The three key approaches used and discussed throughout the book are "questions," "phrases," and "note-taking." Asking questions is the most potent strategy for seeking information and expressing doubts to gain clarification in gaining further knowledge of a young person's problems. Questions help parents to unearth the layers of issues and the mind-set that encapsulates the young person. In this book, questioning involves open-ended, problem-solving, and critical-thinking questions. These methods are all used to solve the situations. Asking questions releases information that might have been withheld from parents until that moment. One question naturally leads to another. Discussing how situations started is the first step in resolution. This process will encourage a healthy conversation. Positive youth development will include habits needed for growth and skill-building. It may consist of educational support, mentorship, and access to resources encouraging personal and academic growth. Questioning may help to change their negative perceptions of themselves into a more positive outlook on their life. These questions can bring clarity during the dark and uncertain days. Questioning will help the parent and young person clarify their situation. The Chapters encourage talking and using the phrases to reduce the stigma that surrounds death by suicide. Asking these questions or saying the phrases is like adding sprinkles to a cream cake! The changing moods of young people can be quite worrying for parents watching. One day, their attitude and countenance can be good, and within hours, the young person can become withdrawn and non-communicative. Consider these actions as usual. Parents can use the questions, phrases, and note-taking to compile the analysis of their child's well-being.

Significance of empowerment in preventing suicide among youths

It is time to empower our young people to prevent suicide among youth! Empowerment requires a diverse approach involving education awareness, health support systems, and environments that encourage healthy habits. Stopping both physical bullying and cyber bullying is imperative. Schools, colleges, and community outlets should implement regular anti-bullying programs. These centres of learning must be safe and supportive because the effects of bullying can impact young people's mental well-being. Throughout the education and awareness programs, it's crucial to ensure that young people have convenient access to counselling and mental health services. Freely distribute flyers, booklets, info graphics, pens, and key rings containing telephone numbers and website details. These support groups and agencies will offer confidential helplines and counselling services. Promote youth suicide prevention by using online resources, websites, and apps. These websites may have self-help tools that provide mental health resources and links to other websites and books. Implementing various methods should foster open discussions about preventing youth suicide and mental health, eliminating stigma, and establishing a supportive environment.

Young people should feel free from judgment regarding their actions. Peer support programs are an excellent way of establishing peer support networks and mentorship programs for young people. Trained mentors in youth suicide prevention will offer young people the opportunity to seek advice and guidance. Parents must get involved in education awareness programs, seminars, and workshops to empower young people. Parents should provide support and a listening ear when children need to offload their concerns. Parents must constantly engage to deliver the links between the home, school, and support groups.

Empowerment is very significant in changing the mental well-being of young people. Words are so powerful. Freely distribute flyers, booklets, info graphics, pens, and key rings containing telephone numbers and website details. Parents must use words of affirmation when speaking to their children.

CONCLUSION

A daily dosage of cheerful words that pave a path of encouragement would bring miracles. So, parents say words of life and words of hope. Teachers and community youth leaders need to have regular training sessions to keep up to date with youth culture, the trends, and the warning signs that would identify youth suicide. When these signs are recognised, parents can provide immediate support. Their training will reinforce methods of observation, engaging conversations, and using questions to understand the young people in their care. Parents can encourage their children to develop healthy daily exercise habits, eat a balanced diet, and sleep well. Reducing gaming and online social networking time would contribute to better mental well-being. This healthy lifestyle is something that parents need to promote and uphold. The mental health awareness in preventing suicide among youth is a big topic. Young people living in supportive homes are less likely to engage in risky behaviours such as substance abuse, violence, or delinquency.

Emphasise the need for increased awareness and education

Religions and social beliefs form the melting pot of our metropolitan society. Different cultures have their stance and ideologies about death by suicide. Cultural and religious beliefs may differ from one region of a town to another. You can read the differences of opinions in online conversations and Quora debates. Debates about life, death, and what happens after death are hot topics. There are lots of differences with not a lot of common ground, so these differences make the teaching of preventing youth suicide so debatable. The negative perceptions about the topic can cause distress and unrest.

Let's advocate for change and increased awareness. Put aside our differences and hold regular programs and education seminars online to help to overcome this. As a result of applying the principles outlined in this book, rifting families can discuss and resolve issues. To address the rise in youth suicide, we need to openly and frequently discuss the subject. Online youth forums should discuss, debate, and petition to have more resources and seminars for preventative methods. Schools, community youth institutes, and colleges should have regular open discussions or online forums where young people and adults can express themselves. A forum specially designed for this topic should be a safe platform where young people ask questions and challenge other young people's problems and perceptions.

Discuss the roles of families in supporting at-risk youth

The role of the family, which involves parents, siblings, and close family members, is central to the support that to youth who are contemplating death by suicide. Their home should be a safe space where they feel understood, valued, and encouraged during their times of vulnerability. Families provide the ideal emotional, social, and psychological nurturing and growth conditions. The role of the family is essential in building the child's confidence during their early years of development. Young people are significantly influenced by what they see, so the parental role model is crucial. Parents would be the first point of contact for schools or health professionals should any matter arise. Supporting children and adolescents relies on emphasizing the central role of the family unit. Parents should create a supportive home environment. The young person's well-being and the way that they communicate stems from what they have learned from their parents. On the contrary, some young people have a good family upbringing, but they choose the paths of substance abuse, alcohol consumption, or becoming sexually promiscuous. A positive family environment contributes to a young person's resilience and ability to cope with challenges.

The local community has a significant place in society. Young people learn a lot from others in their local community. Young people grow and are nurtured in community youth clubs and sports venues. Regular forums will not be endorsing the actions of death by suicide, but on the contrary, it will be a safe platform where young people can ask or answer questions about the prevention of youth suicide. The purpose will be to challenge young people's societal problems and find possible solutions. Communication between children and young adults will encourage others to join the debate. Through healthy relationships, young people will cultivate empathy, communication skills, and the ability to form positive connections, which are crucial for their social and emotional development. Watch your children look at their habits and analyse their behaviour and mental well-being. Parents and educators must teach young people how to develop resilience and effective coping mechanisms. Through positive talk and self-affirmation, young people will become stronger mentally. Young people must learn techniques to help manage stress, improve focus, and build emotional resilience. When they have to battle with the difficulties of life, then the resilience that they have learned will help them in the future. The young person will bounce back from setbacks more readily.

Discuss the roles of schools in supporting at-risk youth

The roles of schools are crucial in supporting the prevention of youth suicide. The young person spends most of their day in the school building. Teachers and other school staff are often the first to observe the behaviour of young people. They can identify students through their academic performance and attendance records and monitor changes in behaviour. They can spot social and peer issues. School teachers and staff can collaborate with parents and raise awareness of unusual behaviour. This collaboration will entail organising school meetings to facilitate referrals to external healthcare providers. Schools can be supportive by creating a nurturing environment where young people can speak with designated staff about their problems. Schools can provide free school meals to young people whose families are experiencing social and economic factors that can impede their health and well-being. A warm school meal every day will help to sustain them. Most schools have counsellors who offer guidance for coping with emotional and mental health issues. The school counsellors can implement intervention strategies for at-risk youth during their academic day. They can provide resources and help for the families of these students so that plans are in place within their homes. Teachers and staff can empower young people by providing vital resources that would educate them about youth suicide prevention. A course may offer an opportunity for skill-building and personal development.

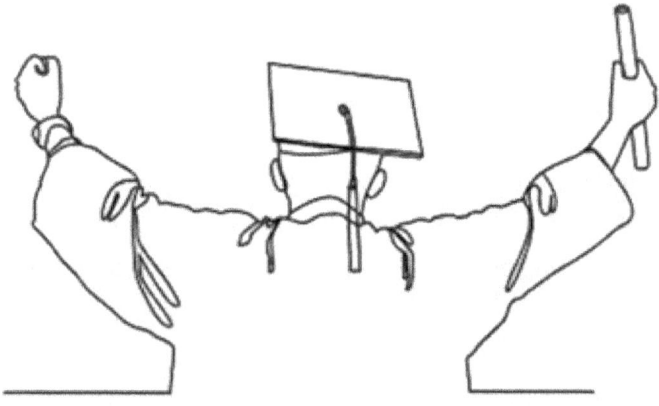

Discuss the roles of healthcare providers in supporting at-risk youth

Healthcare providers can support young people to prevent suicide in several ways. Healthcare providers are the essential links that collaborate with schools, community youth organisations, and social services to support these young people. By identifying the health issues of young people, healthcare providers can create a plan of action for the health issues they are experiencing. Ensuring they receive regular check-ups, nutritional guidance, and support to improve their overall health and well-being. By providing services for their physical needs, healthcare providers will address their mental health needs.

Specialised psychologists, psychiatrists, counsellors, and social workers will be accessible to young people as part of the initiative to prevent youth suicide. These healthcare providers will deliver preventative suicide care through workshops, seminars, and resources supplied to the at-risk youth, the school, or their families. Healthcare professionals provide the necessary resources and support for substance abuse treatment for young people.

Statistical evidence

The data indicates an increase in suicide rates within this specific demographic. Here are some organisations that regularly release statistical reports and sources offering global figures and data concerning youth suicide:

The World Health Organization (WHO) consistently issues worldwide reports on suicide statistics, offering detailed information on youth suicide rates categorised by country and region. These comprehensive reports from the WHO offer profound insights into not just the rates but also the risk factors and strategies for preventing suicide.

The Centers for Disease Control and Prevention (CDC) in the United States provides comprehensive data and reports specifically focused on youth suicide rates and evolving trends. These reports emphasize various risk factors, demographics, and regional differences associated with youth suicide.

UK's Office for National Statistics (ONS) provides detailed data on suicide rates, including breakdowns by age groups. UNICEF periodically publishes reports concerning the well-being of children and adolescents, encompassing mental health statistics and indicators that shed light on youth suicide rates across diverse geographical regions.

The Global Burden of Disease Study (GBD), overseen by the Institute for Health Metrics and Evaluation (IHME), publishes extensive insights into worldwide health patterns, encompassing detailed statistics on suicide rates across various age brackets. Consistently gathering and sharing information regarding youth suicide rates, risk factors, and preventive strategies on a global scale, these outlets offer critical insights to policymakers, healthcare experts, and researchers engaged in mental health and suicide prevention efforts. It is advisable to consult their most recent reports and publications for the most up-to-date and precise data. The author believes this book will save lives and bring about change. This book is simple; even a child can read it and gain more knowledge about the prevention of suicide and attempted suicide.

We, as parents and guardians, need to approach the prevention of youth suicide with practical, grassroots strategies. The strategies are brief, so readers can quickly read what they need. The advice is accessible and valuable, and parents and young adults will understand and follow the processes of making a change. The impact that this book will have on families is enormous. It's a game-changer.

Schools need to change the approach by openly addressing the topic of death by suicide, which is currently not spoken about. The national curriculum is the standard by which the schools follow. The "Prevention of Youth Suicide" is a topic that schools should have as a part of their curriculum. Even though it does not have the same status as the core disciplines, this topic is a compulsory need. Primary schools should run a workshop every term tackling this problem. Secondary schools should also run workshops and have open discussions every term.

Additionally, secondary schools should offer a qualification in this subject. "The Prevention of Youth Suicide" can be students' main subject or study module. The government ought to amend the National Curriculum to reflect this. BTEC, GCSE, and Nationals should be courses of study for "The Prevention of Youth Suicide." After studying this subject in school, students can pursue a career as a counsellor or a coach.

In college, "The Prevention of Youth Suicide" should be a compulsory module of study. As a study discipline, it could be part of social studies, counselling, and coaching. Workshops should run every term for the students, along with open discussions. Death by suicide is a taboo subject with negative perceptions. Many people shun away from it, either refusing to talk about it or making fun of some aspect of it. People tackle problems and issues in different ways.

"Let's talk about the prevention of Youth Suicide." Schedule a platform, invite your guests, and start talking. Many situations trigger negative actions for a child or a young adult, which is the primary reason for writing this book with many questions about varying situations. These situations stir up the past and bring a flood of emotions to the forefront of the mind, and the child or young person may be afraid of them or unable to resolve them alone. Let's resolve youth problems.

A message of HOPE

Whatever your reason for reading this book, I hope it has been of great value. I hope that together, we have sowed the seeds of hope and that you will have a harvest of joy in time. Let's continue to help young people by encouraging as many young people and adults as possible to share this book. Please share this book with your friends and your enemies. Consider the following: Some people are your enemy because of how they feel about their lives, and they have seen that your life is following, and they deflect their actions in defence of their inner feelings. Yes, this is deep. These people you love from a distance, I will call them your distance acquaintances.

Please email 20 friends and two distant acquaintances. Send a WhatsApp message to 20 friends and two distant acquaintances. Send a Discord shout-out to 20 friends and two distant acquaintances; Send a Twitter message to 20 friends and two distant acquaintances. Send a Facebook message to 20 friends and two distant acquaintances. Please message your local school requesting that they stock this book. Please message your local college asking that they stock this book. Please message your local library requesting that they stock this book.

It would have been worth writing this book if the author had helped one young person. Let's work together to get this book out to young people globally. The author asks the readers to pledge to take action to support suicide prevention efforts.

For everyone who has encountered such a painful tragedy, my thoughts and prayers go out to you.

My prayer: I pray that what you have experienced is something that you will gain strength from. Every disappointment in life is God's appointment, meaning it's a chance to do something great with you and for you. I pray that every dark and probing comment you hear, and every snide remark will wash off your back. I pray that each day from now on, you will become like a rock, unstoppable. You will not be a victim of life because this is your year, your month of change. You will overcome, and I pray that you are more robust and become reciprocal of your mind. I pray that all feelings of numbness in your body will disappear when you read these words. You will become victorious in life.

I pray for the restoration of your body and the repair of your mind. I pray that the dark clouds surrounding you will part so you can see the colourful day. Yes, you have experienced the loss of a loved one, and now you are going to be bold and more assertive. I pray that you decide to help others who have gone through similar circumstances. So that in helping others, you will help yourself. These are the blessings that I pray for you. Amen.

Connect with the Author

Death by suicide has a stigma attached to it. The reason why I wrote this book was to create a social forum. Young people, adolescents, friends, and parents can talk and discuss Youth Suicide Prevention. Local communities, school children, and charity groups can initiate forums that foster conversations evolving into debates. As a result of the debates, many young people and adults will find resolutions to their problems. Resolutions will be on the platform for all to see. Parents can use these resolutions in their homes with their children. Friends can use the resolutions with their friends. Family members can use these resolutions with other family members. Teachers can use these resolutions in their classrooms. Teachers can also use the resolutions as a point on their agenda for school staff meetings. If you're interested in joining our Youth Suicide Prevention Forum, please send an email to:

enquiries@nature-restores.com

Are you interested in receiving a monthly Newsletter about Youth Suicide Prevention? Please email your name and send a quick message to:

info@nature-restores.com

The Nature-Restores team will add your details to the mailing list. Thank you for being willing to change a young person's life.

admin@nature-restores.com

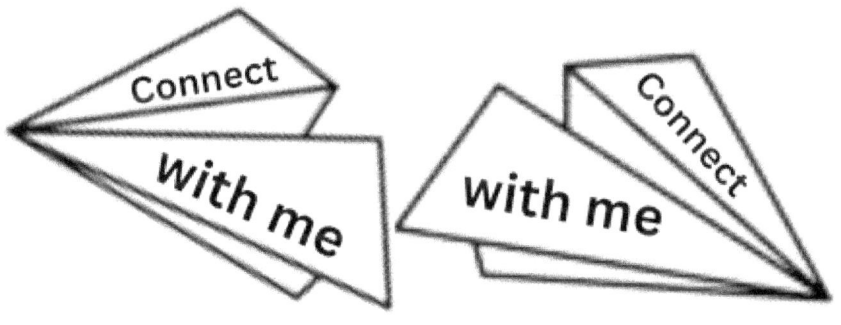

Notes

Plan of action

12

Youth Suicide Prevention help and support

Support Worldwide

https://www.crisistextline.org/text-us/

- United States: Text 741741
- Canada: Text 686868
- United Kingdom: Text 85258
- Ireland: Text 50808

https://findahelpline.com/
Find a help line have suicide prevention helplines in the United Kingdom. In the United States they have a suicide, depression and anxiety helpline. In India and in Canada they have a suicide prevention helplines.

https://help.befrienders.org/
Befrienders Worldwide provide confidential support to people in emotional crisis or distress, or those close to them.

https://blog.opencounseling.com/suicide-hotlines/ International Suicide Hotlines.

https://www.iasp.info/ International Association for Suicide Prevention.

https://www.stompoutbullying.org/international-suicide-prevention-resource Stomp Out Bullying. End the Hate....Change the Culture. International Suicide Prevention Resource.

http://www.suicide.org/international-suicide-hotlines.html Suicide Prevention, Awareness and Support.

Support in the United Kingdom

https://www.gov.uk/government/collections/suicide-prevention-resources-and-guidance Suicide prevention, help for local authorities and public sector groups with resources and guidance.

https://www.mind.org.uk/ Suicide is the biggest killer of men and boys aged 9 to 50.

https://nspa.org.uk/about-us/ National Suicide Prevention Alliance.

https://www.papyrus-uk.org/ PAPYRUS Prevention of Young Suicide.

https://www.samaritans.org/about-samaritans/our-organisation/national-suicide-prevention-alliance/ The Samaritans: suicide prevention alliance.

YOUTH SUICIDE PREVENTION HELP AND SUPPORT

DEAL: developing listening skills QR Code1

Samaritans' strategy: Tackling suicide together QR Code2

Support in the United States of America

https://www.dcyf.wa.gov/safety/youth-suicide-prevention Washington State department of Children, Youth and Families. Youth Suicide Prevention.

https://www.defense.gov/Spotlights/Suicide-Prevention/ U.S Department of defence suicide prevention.

https://www.health.ny.gov/prevention/injury_prevention/children/fact_sheets/10-19_years/suicide_prevention_10-19_years.htm Suicide Prevention of Children ages 10 -19 years.

https://www.aap.org/en/patient-care/blueprint-for-youth-suicide-prevention/ Suicide: Blueprint for Youth Suicide Prevention

https://www.thetrevorproject.org/get-help/ Telephone number 866-488-7386. The Trevor Project's mission is to end suicide among LGBTQ young people in the USA.

https://youth.gov/youth-topics/youth-suicide-prevention Preventing Youth Suicide.

YOUTH SUICIDE PREVENTION HELP AND SUPPORT

13

Resources

A look at the latest suicide data and change over the last decade | KFF. (2023, August 21). KFF. https://www.kff.org/mental-health/issue-brief/a-look-at-the-latest-suicide-data-and-change-over-the-last-decade/

Can - Quick search results | Oxford English Dictionary. (n.d.). https://www.oed.com/search/dictionary/?scope=Entries&q=CAN+

Chris. (2023, October 10). *What is low mood? 7 Great Tips to Breaking Out | Build Me Up.* Build Me Up. https://www.buildmeup.uk/what-is-low-mood/

1. Communication Skills: 18 Strategies to communicate Better. (n.d.-b). https://www.betterup.com/blog/effective-strategies-to-improve-your-communication-skills

Compas, B. E., Orosan, P. G., & Grant, K. E. (1993). *Adolescent stress and coping: implications for psychopathology during adolescence. Journal of Adolescence,* 16(3), 331–349. https://doi.org/10.1006/jado.1993.1028

Dattani, S., Rodés-Guirao,L., Ritchie, H., Roser., M, &Ortiz-Ospina, E.

(2023) - *"Suicides".* Published online at OurWorldInData.org. Retrieved from:

RESOURCES

'https://ourworldindata.org/suicide' Online resource accessed 1.12.2023

DEAL: developing listening skills. (n.d.-a). Samaritans. https://www.samaritans.org/scotland/how-we-can-help/schools/deal/deal-resources/connecting-others/listening-skills/

Facts about suicide | Suicide Prevention | CDC. (n.d.). https://www.cdc.gov/suicide/facts/index.html

Gilbert, K. (2012). *The neglected role of positive emotion in adolescent psychopathology.* Clinical Psychology Review, 32(6), 467–481. https://doi.org/10.1016/j.cpr.2012.05.005

https://www.kff.org/mental-health/issue-brief/a-look-at-the-latest-suicide-data-and-change-over-the-last-decade/

Mais, R. N. E. J. a. D. (2022, September 5). *Suicides in England and Wales - Office for National Statistics.* https://www.ons.gov.uk/peoplepopulationandcommunity/birthsdeathsandmarriages/deaths/bulletins/suicidesintheunitedkingdom/2021registrations

Panchal, N & Saunders, S. (2023). *A Look at the Latest Suicide Data and Change Over the Last Decade.* Online resource accessed 1.12.2023

Problem_1 noun - Definition, pictures, pronunciation and usage notes | Oxford Advanced Learner's Dictionary at OxfordLearnersDictionaries.com. (n.d.-a). https://www.oxfordlearnersdictionaries.com/us/definition/english/problem_1

Rogers, K. (Sept, 2022) *"Debunking myths about suicide helps encourage compassion and understanding."* Retrieved from: https://edition.cnn.com/2022/09/10/health/suicide-myths-facts-prevention-wellness Online resource accessed 1.12.2023

Samaritans' strategy: Tackling suicide together. (n.d.). Samaritans. https://www.samaritans.org/scotland/about-samaritans/our-organisation/our-strategy/

Spitz, A., Aebi, M., Metzke, C. W., Walitza, S., & Steinhausen, H. (2022). *Stability and change in a predictive model of emotional and behavioural problems from early adolescence to middle adulthood.* Journal of Psychiatric Research, 151, 8–16. https://doi.org/10.1016/j.jpsychires.2022.03.029

The Creativity post | Requisites for Learning: The 5 Rs. (2021, October 12). The Creativity Post. https://www.creativitypost.com/article/requisites-for-learning-the-5-rs

United We Care. (2023, October 19). *10 useful tips to tackle Claustrophobia. United We Care | a Super App for Mental Wellness.* https://www.unitedwecare.com/10-useful-tips-to-tackle-claustrophobia/

Epilogue

A Call to Collective Action

The world that we live in is ever-changing. We have seen pandemics come and go. We have embraced AI's impact on every aspect of society, from the fields to the classrooms. AI is making our lives easier. The shifting patterns of youth culture show that the minds of young people are more glued to their screens. Their conversations centre on their screen interactions. Now, gaming replaces going outdoors, and meeting up and socialising occur within an online gaming environment.

The minds of the developing young person have become more introverted. The experimental, curious, outgoing, fresh air-breathing extrovert mind has disappeared. The capsule of online games and forums creates a society of expression dictated by internet followers or influencers. There has been statistical evidence of the increased shift and the change in the cases of death by suicide by young people. Depression and mental health increasingly pose a growing issue, obscuring the mind with a dark cloud. The parental struggle to accurately diagnose their child is another crucial determining factor.

Each chapter gave parents insights into the educational structure, offering model questions and answers to initiate conversations and discussions. The responsibility rests with the young person, their parents, family members, teachers, community members, and policymakers. After reading and digesting the discourse, circulate and promote the reading of this book; send the web details as a link to all who would benefit from the value it brings. The cases of suicide around your community may reduce after the awareness and prevention education are shared.

As we close the chapter of this book and our pursuit of youth suicide prevention, it's not the end but the beginning of the quest. The journey through this book was a testament to the complexity and gravity of the challenges surrounding youth suicide. It illuminated the intricate web of factors of health struggles, societal pressures, trauma, and isolation. Our discussions delved into raising awareness, eliminating stigma, and providing accessible resources. We explored the power of early intervention, fostering positive environments, and empowering youth to seek help without fear or shame.

This epilogue isn't a conclusion; it's a call to action, reminding us to continue our efforts. It's a commitment to continue the conversation, to advocate tirelessly for mental health support, and to create environments where every young person feels valued and supported. We can change our communities by joining hands, raising our voices, and advocating for change. We can make a difference.

Let this book catalyze action. Gears work by interlocking together, forming a mechanism that drives motion. In the same way, our continuous learning and tireless efforts are crucial to ensuring that young lives are safeguarded from the tragedy of suicide. Let's persist in acquiring knowledge and dedicating ourselves to this cause to create a world where the value of every young life is recognised and preserved. Our interaction, our interlocking, will serve to power one another.

Thank you for reading this book. Now, let us march forward, united in our commitment to Youth Suicide Prevention.

With much love and HOPE,

Author Odelyn Smith

Afterword

Embracing Hope - A Journey in Youth Suicide Prevention

As we conclude the book but not the subject, we can reflect on the more acute issues that have arisen from the discourse of this book. I hope this book has been an inspiration and aspiration, a light in a dark place or a lighthouse guiding against impending doom. Whatever your reasons, I believe that the following key points summarise the core knowledge gleaned from the pages of this book:

Awareness and education are paramount in our mission to diffuse youth suicide. The book helped parents identify initial signs and behaviours, which is the knowledge we all need. Spread the word and spread the hope that has grown from reading the book. Onwards and forwards should be our continuing motto. Through our awareness and education, we should impact our schools, communities, and our families.

Normalising conversations about youth mental health is something that we all have to work towards. Stigma still hangs over the subject, and those who suffer often go undetected. Eradicating the stigma attached to seeking help and talking about struggles is pivotal. More importantly, accepting and believing the young person wants to end their life by suicide are the first steps towards restoration and healing.

Accessing the support services is crucial in the fight against Youth Suicide Prevention. Parents must contact their doctor or a health professional to do the initial assessment; they must promptly contact mental health services, hotlines, support groups, and peer-to-peer initiatives. Maintaining a productive network between the services is another battle. The collaboration between parents, family members, school teachers, and health and mental health professionals is an enormous team. Their partnership is essential in saving the life of a young person.

Promoting positive environments and positive vibes is vital for young people to feel safe and nurtured. Fostering nurturing and inclusive environments where young individuals feel safe, supported, and valued is crucial. Positive connections with support agencies and a sense of belonging are protective factors against suicide risk. Demonstrating positive vibes around vulnerable young people helps.

Give a voice to those who have overcome teenage suicide ideation, and they can share an edited version of their struggles and how they overcame them. Their stories can be a powerful testimony, showing hope and inspiration to other struggling young people. The stories will also show that it is possible to be successful in the end.

The message of hope is the ultimate goal. The pathways of help will secure the young person, and through conversations and resources, the objective is to nurture and build resilience to life's challenges. This journey is ongoing. This chapter must never be closed. The journey is not an easy one in preventing youth suicide, and it will take stamina, determination, and the application of numerous prevention strategies to continue.

Thank you for joining this discourse and your dedication to such a worthy cause. This parental guide, teamed with your commitment to Youth Suicide Prevention, is a lifeline to countless young people.

With hope,

Author Odelyn Smith

About the Author

As a globally recognised educator, accomplished author, astute business strategist, and innovative designer, Odelyn Smith brings a wealth of expertise and insight to the domains of education, business, and design. With a robust portfolio spanning diverse sectors, Odelyn has established a formidable reputation for delivering transformative solutions and driving impactful change across borders.

With an unwavering commitment to education, Odelyn has empowered countless individuals worldwide through pioneering teaching methodologies and influential written works. As an author, Odelyn Smith's publications resonate globally, offering invaluable insights into well-being, design principles, and educational paradigms, fostering growth and innovation.

As a seasoned business strategist, Odelyn leverages unparalleled expertise to guide organisations toward success in today's dynamic market landscape. Known for visionary thinking and a strategic approach, Odelyn Smith has helped numerous businesses navigate challenges, optimise operations, and achieve sustainable growth.

Moreover, Odelyn is a visionary designer, blending creativity with functionality to craft compelling visual narratives and innovative solutions that captivate audiences and drive engagement.

Also by Odelyn Smith

My work is who I am...

Changing Fear to Peace

Kindly buy my book on Amazon and share your thoughts with a review.

https://www.amazon.co.uk/Changing-Fear-PEACE-Cultivate-Resilience/dp/1739586905

My website

https://nature-restores.com

   Advertise with me enquiries@nature-restores.com

Please subscribe to my email list admin@nature-restores.com

Business enquiries info@nature-restores.com

My website

https://ostutoring.com

Advertise with me enquiries@ostutoring.com

Please subscribe to my email list admin@ostutoring.com

Business enquiries info@ostutoring.com

Social Media Links
YouTube Channel: Global Education Academy of Restoration GEAR @GloEduAcaofRestGEAR

Please consider subscribing to my YouTube channel, sharing the content, and giving it a thumbs-up.

Social Media Links
YouTube Channel: Global Wholesaler @globalwholesaler

Feel free to subscribe to my YouTube channel, share the content, and give it a thumbs up!

Social Media Links

Ask me questions on Quora: https://naturerestorescom.quora.com/

Ask me a question?

Social Media Links

Ask me questions on Quora: https://ostutoringcom.quora.com/

Ask me a question?

Connect with me 🌍

Fashion Designer https://www.odelynsmith.com/

Online Store

My Etsy Shop Educator Designer: https://www.etsy.com/uk/shop/EducatorDesigner?ref=profile_header

Coming Soon

https://www.nutritionrestores.com/

Blog Explore Nutrition Restores for valuable insights on cultivating a healthy lifestyle, expert gym tips, and comprehensive education on overall well-being. Empower yourself with knowledge for a healthier you!

www.ingramcontent.com/pod-product-compliance
Lightning Source LLC
Chambersburg PA
CBHW061330040426
42444CB00011B/2855